RIPPLE EFFECT

REBECCA JEAN BERGQUIST

ISBN: 979-8-218-27726-0

Printed in the United States of America

TABLE OF CONTENTS

Part 1
Navigating Setbacks

Chapter 1
A Promising Start

Growing up, I always believed that life doesn't always give you happy endings as it appears in the movies. For me, life is a journey of rollercoasters, where you are bound to go through ups and downs. At times, you find yourself at the lowest point, while at others, you soar to the seventh sky. Regardless of the phase you find yourself in, it's important to control your emotions and not allow them to dictate your actions. Decision-making led by emotions can often lead to undesirable outcomes. The key is to remain mindful and accept everything as part of reality.

My childhood was blissful, filled with sweet nurturing and care. I grew up in the beautiful state of Idaho, surrounded by nature's wonders. The vast landscapes and majestic mountains became my playground, fueling my imagination and sense of adventure. I was fortunate to be raised in a loving and supportive family, where optimism and a zest for life were instilled in me from a young age.

I was always an optimistic person, a true flower child. Even as a child, I possessed a deep appreciation for the world around me. I spent countless hours exploring the outdoors, captivated by the beauty of nature. I found solace in the melody of birdsong, the whispering of leaves, and the gentle touch of a summer breeze. My imagination soared as I weaved stories and created fantastical worlds in my mind. I was a dreamer, finding joy in the simplest of pleasures.

As I grew older, my optimistic outlook on life remained intact. I approached each day with a sense of wonder and curiosity, eager to discover what new adventures awaited me. While some might have seen challenges as obstacles, I saw them as opportunities for growth and self-discovery. I believed in the power of resilience and the ability to overcome any hurdle that life threw my way.

Finally, the day arrived when I stood on the precipice of realizing my dreams. Graduation day from high school marked the beginning of a new chapter in my life. As I walked across the stage to receive my diploma, I felt proud of myself. The applause and cheers of my family and friends reverberated in my ears, reminding me of the support and love that surrounded me.

I had no intention to join the Air Force until my graduation in 2000. Until an year later, when a pivotal event ignited my passion to join the Air Force—September 11, 2001. The tragic events of that day shook the world to its core, leaving an indelible mark on my young mind. Witnessing the bravery and sacrifice of the men and women in uniform, who selflessly rushed to aid those in need, stirred something within me. It was at that moment that I knew I wanted to serve my country and make a difference in the world.

The decision to join the Air Force became my driving force. I was determined to contribute to the noble cause of protecting and defending our nation. I immersed myself in physical training, preparing my body and mind for the demanding rigors of military life. The thought of dressing yourself in the uniform and standing shoulder to shoulder with fellow patriots filled me with a sense of pride and purpose.

Days turned into months, and months turned into years as I diligently worked towards my goal. I maintained a strict fitness routine, pushing my limits to surpass the expectations set before me. I studied tirelessly, absorbing every piece of information related to the Air Force, its values, and its missions. My dedication was unwavering, fueled by an unyielding determination to succeed.

However, fate had a different plan in store for me. It was during the summer before I was set to embark on my military journey that tragedy struck. On a seemingly ordinary day, my life took an unexpected turn. I found myself in a car accident that would change the course of my destiny.

The accident was a blur of screeching tires, shattered glass, and the sound of twisting metal. In an instant, my dreams of joining the Air Force collided with the harsh reality of a broken back. The pain was excruciating, both physically and emotionally. As I lay there, immobilized and vulnerable, I knew that my path had taken an unforeseen detour.

Days turned into weeks as I grappled with the aftermath of the accident. The news that followed was devastating—I was disqualified from joining the Air Force due to my injury. The weight of that realization crashed down upon me, threatening to shatter the optimism that had defined my spirit. It felt as though the sky had darkened, and my dreams had been ripped away from me. Thus, I decided to return to Idaho, my hometown, so that I could be close to my family and friends in such crucial times.

It was in the depths of despair that I found solace in the support of my family and friends. They stood by my side, offering their unwavering love and encouragement. Their belief in me rekindled the flame of hope within my heart. They reminded me that setbacks are not the end of the road but merely detours leading to new paths.

In the midst of my disappointment and frustration, I made a conscious choice to channel my energy into seeking alternative ways to make a difference. I began to explore different avenues where I could still serve and impact lives in a meaningful way. It was during this time that an opportunity arose—a chance to become a nanny for a Wall Street family in New Jersey.

Embracing the unexpected turn of events, I packed my bags and embarked on a new adventure. New Jersey welcomed me with its bustling streets and towering skyscrapers, a stark contrast to the serene landscapes of my childhood. I immersed myself in the role of a caregiver, nurturing and guiding the children entrusted to my care. Though the path diverged from my original plan, I discovered that making a difference didn't require a uniform or a rank. It could be found in the small moments, in shaping young minds and instilling values that would resonate throughout their lives.

As the days turned into weeks and then months, I found a renewed sense of purpose. The journey I had embarked upon may have been different from what I had initially thought to be, but it was no less meaningful. I witnessed the growth and development of the children I cared for, celebrating their milestones and offering guidance along the way. Each day brought new challenges and triumphs, reminding me of the impact I could have on the lives of others.

The rejection from the Air Force had tested my resilience and determination, but it had also opened my eyes to new possibilities. Life had presented me with a detour, but I was determined to make it a remarkable journey nonetheless. I learned to adapt and embrace the unexpected, discovering strength within myself that I hadn't known existed.

Looking back, I realized that the accident, though devastating, had taught me invaluable lessons. It taught me the power of acceptance, of acknowledging that life doesn't always unfold according to our plans. It taught me the importance of resilience and the ability to find new paths when the old ones close. Most importantly, it taught me that setbacks are not the end of the story but opportunities for growth and self-discovery.

As I reflected on my journey, I couldn't help but feel a sense of gratitude. The accident had shattered my dreams, but it had also allowed me to uncover new passions and explore uncapped territories. I learned that life's detours often lead us to places we never could have imagined, introducing us to people and experiences that shape us in profound ways.

As I stood at the crossroads, contemplating my next steps, I felt a renewed sense of purpose burning within me. The rejection from the Air Force was not the end of my story; it was merely the beginning of a new chapter—one filled with unexpected twists, renewed purpose, and a determination to rise above the challenges that lay ahead.

With unwavering determination, I vowed to forge my own path, guided by the lessons learned and the unwavering support of my loved ones. I knew that the road ahead would not be easy, but I was prepared to face the obstacles with courage and resilience. The chapter of rebuilding my life and self-discovery for which I was ready to embrace it with open arms.

As the sun set on that eventful day, I felt a sense of peace wash over me. The darkness that had overshadowed my dreams was slowly dissipating, making way for a new dawn. The promise of a promising start lay ahead, and I was determined to seize it with every fiber of my being. Life had tested me, but I refused to let it break me. I was ready to embark on the next phase of my journey, armed with hope, resilience, and an unwavering belief in the power of second chances.

I took a deep breath, allowing the fresh air to fill my lungs as I stood at the crossroads of my life. The accident had changed everything, altering the trajectory of my dreams and aspirations. But I refused to let it define me. Instead, I chose to see it as an opportunity for growth, a chance to discover new passions and carve out a different path.

As I settled into my role as a nanny in New Jersey, I found solace in the smiles and laughter of the children under my care. Each day brought its own set of challenges and joys, reminding me of the resilience and adaptability I possessed within. I poured my heart into nurturing and guiding them, knowing that I was making a difference in their lives, even if it wasn't in the way I had initially envisioned.

Time passed, and as the seasons changed, so did my perspective. I realized that life's detours were not roadblocks but invitations to explore uncharted territories. It was during this period of self-discovery that I found a newfound love for music and began exploring my creative side. I picked up a guitar and poured my emotions into heartfelt melodies, finding solace in the harmonies that echoed through my soul. Music became my sanctuary, a place where I could express the depths of my emotions without uttering a single word.

Through music, I discovered a strength I hadn't known existed within me. It became my therapy, allowing me to process the pain and heartache that lingered from the accident. Each string of the guitar served as a release, freeing me from the shackles of my past and propelling me toward a future filled with hope and possibility.

As the melody of my life began to take shape, I found myself longing for a sense of purpose beyond the confines of the nanny role. The desire to contribute to something greater than myself burned within me, urging me to explore new avenues of service. With an open heart and mind, I delved into volunteer work, lending a helping hand to various charitable organizations. Whether it was feeding the homeless or supporting local initiatives, I discovered the profound impact that small acts of kindness could have on individuals and communities.

As I immersed myself in these experiences, a new sense of purpose bloomed within me. I realized that serving others, even in the smallest of ways, brought me immense joy and fulfillment. It was a humbling reminder that life's purpose is not solely defined by the path we initially set out on but rather by the impact we have on the lives of those around us.

With each passing day, I continued to rebuild my spirit, piece by piece. I discovered the power of self-care, dedicating time to nourish my mind, body, and soul. I surrounded myself with positive influences and sought out mentors who could guide me along this new journey. Their wisdom and guidance provided the support I needed to navigate the challenges that arose.

As I continued to grow and evolve, the pain of the accident began to lose its grip on me. It no longer defined who I was but became a chapter in my story, a testament to the resilience of the human spirit. I realized that my dreams were not confined to a specific career or role but encompassed the ability to make a positive impact wherever life led me.

The journey had been difficult, filled with moments of doubt and uncertainty. But through it all, I learned to trust in the process and have faith in my own strength. I had discovered that setbacks were not failures but opportunities for growth and transformation.

As I looked back at the young girl who had once dreamed of joining the Air Force, I couldn't help but smile. Life had taken me on a different path, but I had embraced it wholeheartedly. I had grown in ways I never thought possible, and my sense of purpose had been reignited.

As the sun dipped below the horizon, casting a warm glow over the world around me, I felt a profound sense of gratitude. Gratitude for the experiences that had shaped me, for the resilience that had carried me through the darkest of times, and for the unwavering support of those who had believed in me.

The journey was far from over, but as I stood there, I knew I was no longer defined by the accident. I was a survivor, a dreamer, and a believer in the power of second chances. With every beat of my heart, I vowed to embrace the promising start that awaited me, to live each day with intention, and to never lose sight of the incredible strength that resided within me.

As the night sky unfolded, twinkling with the promise of endless possibilities, I took a step forward, ready to embrace the next chapter of my life with open arms. The road ahead was uncertain, but I knew that as long as I stayed true to myself and remained open to the unexpected, I would continue to grow, evolve, and make a difference in the world—one detour at a time.

The days turned into weeks, and the weeks into months, as I continued to navigate the uncharted territory of my post-accident life. With each passing day, I discovered new depths of strength and resilience within myself. I faced moments of doubt and uncertainty, but I refused to let them consume me. Instead, I embraced the challenges as opportunities for growth and self-discovery.

During this time, I found solace in the beauty of nature. Idaho, my hometown, offered a picturesque backdrop for healing and reflection. I would often retreat to the nearby mountains, immersing myself in the tranquility of the forests and the majesty of the peaks. The sound of the wind rustling through the trees and the scent of pine needles in the air reminded me of the resilience of nature itself. It served as a powerful reminder that even in the face of adversity, life finds a way to endure and flourish.

As I continued to heal physically and emotionally, I realized that my dreams and aspirations were not limited to a specific career or path. I yearned for a life filled with purpose and meaning, a life where I could make a positive impact on others. This realization led me to explore different avenues of service and volunteer work.

I became involved in local community initiatives, lending a helping hand wherever it was needed. Whether it was organizing food drives for the less fortunate or participating in environmental conservation projects, I found immense fulfillment in giving back to the community. Through these acts of service, I discovered the power of collective action and the transformative effect it had on both individuals and communities.

One particular experience that left a profound impact on me was volunteering at a local shelter for domestic violence survivors. It was there that I witnessed firsthand the strength and resilience of these individuals, who had overcome unimaginable hardships. Their stories of survival and courage inspired me to become an advocate for those who had experienced trauma and abuse. I realized that my own journey of rebuilding and renewal could serve as a beacon of hope for others going through similar challenges.

In addition to my volunteer work, I also delved deeper into my creative pursuits. Music had always been a source of solace for me, and I decided to take my passion to the next level. I joined a local music group, where I had the opportunity to collaborate with talented musicians and share my original songs with the world. The process of creating music became a cathartic experience, allowing me to express my emotions and connect with others on a deeper level.

As time went on, I began to find my footing in this new chapter of my life. I learned to embrace the uncertainty and embrace the journey of self-discovery. I surrounded myself with a supportive network of friends and family who believed in me and encouraged me to pursue my dreams. Their unwavering belief in my abilities gave me the confidence to take risks and step outside my comfort zone.

Through perseverance and determination, I slowly rebuilt my life. I pursued higher education, enrolling in college courses that aligned with my passions and interests. I embarked on a journey of self-education, devouring books and expanding my knowledge in various fields. I discovered a love for writing, using words as a medium to share my experiences and insights with others.

Along the way, I encountered setbacks and obstacles, but I refused to let them deter me. Each challenge became an opportunity for growth and self-reflection. I learned to embrace failure as a stepping stone to success, understanding that it is through our struggles that we truly learn and evolve.

As I reflect upon that transformative period of my life, I am filled with gratitude. Gratitude for the resilience that allowed me to rise from the ashes of adversity. I am grateful for the unwavering support of my loved ones, who stood by my side throughout the journey. And most importantly, gratitude for the lessons I learned and the person I became in the process.

In the depths of despair, I discovered the strength to rebuild and renew. I found my purpose in serving others, sharing my story, and offering hope to those who may be navigating their own storms. I realized that life's greatest challenges can also be the catalysts for our greatest growth.

As I stand here today, I am no longer defined by the car accident that shattered my dreams. Instead, I am defined by the resilience, determination, and unwavering belief in myself that allowed me to rise above the ashes. The promising start that I once longed for is now a reality as I continue to pursue my passions, make a positive impact, and embrace the beauty of life's unpredictable journey.

And so, as the sun sets on this chapter of my life, I eagerly await the dawn of the next. With renewed hope and a heart filled with gratitude, I am ready to embrace whatever lies ahead, knowing that each step I take is a testament to the strength of the human spirit and the power of resilience.

CHAPTER 2

Trials and Triumphs

Life took an unexpected turn after my decision to leave college and move back to my hometown in Idaho. It was a pivotal moment, and little did I know that this choice would lead me on a rollercoaster journey of trials and triumphs.

Leaving college behind was not an easy decision, but deep down, I knew I needed a change. The dreams of joining the Air Force were fading away, and I felt lost, unsure of my next steps in life. However, I was an optimistic soul, always looking for silver linings in every cloud. Perhaps this detour was meant to redirect my path toward something greater.

Rediscovering My Roots

Back in my hometown, I found solace in familiar surroundings but also a sense of urgency to find my purpose. I started working at a deli, which provided a much-needed source of income. Though it wasn't my dream job, I embraced the opportunity to learn and grow. Life had a way of teaching me valuable lessons, and I soaked them in like a sponge.

As I settled into the routine of working at the deli, memories of my childhood flooded back. I had grown up in Idaho, a place filled with sweet nurturing and care. My childhood had been blissful, and I had always been an optimistic person. I was a flower child, spending my days in nature, playing with animals, and letting my imagination soar.

The decision to leave college wasn't solely due to the rejection from the Air Force. It was more about not feeling like I was headed in the right direction. The Air Force had been an impulse idea fueled by my desire to serve my country after the 9/11 incident. However, fate had different plans, and a car accident changed everything.

The Accident and Its Impact

The car accident was a turning point in my life. I was with my soon-to-be husband at a house party when it occurred. We were arguing over a song, and in the midst of the disagreement, he lost control of the car. The vehicle overturned and landed on a jack truck, narrowly avoiding a fatal outcome. I was not wearing my seatbelt, and it was divine intervention that saved me from tragedy.

The accident resulted in a serious injury - I broke my back. The severity of the injury meant that I was disqualified from joining the Air Force. It was devastating news, but I tried to maintain a positive attitude. I believed that things happened for a reason, and perhaps this accident was a blessing in disguise.

With my dream of joining the Air Force shattered, I needed to find a new path. The rejection left me disappointed, but I couldn't dwell on what could have been. Instead, I focused on what lay ahead and embraced the support from my family during this challenging time.

A New Adventure in Jersey

It was during this phase of recovery that an unexpected opportunity presented itself. My aunt, a talented opera singer, lived in Jersey and invited me to accompany her for a while. It was a spontaneous decision, but my heart told me to take a leap of faith.

Jersey was a completely different world from Idaho, and I found myself in a bustling city surrounded by new sights and sounds. However, adjusting to the fast-paced lifestyle and the crowded streets was not without its challenges. I had to learn to be independent, navigate public transportation, and adapt to a new environment.

During my time in Jersey, I was fortunate enough to land a job as a nanny for a Wall Street family. Caring for someone else's children came with its own set of responsibilities, but I embraced the opportunity to experience life from a different perspective. It wasn't easy for me to adapt to the new surroundings, but I somehow managed to place my foot in this new city.

Embracing Change in Australia

As time went on, my heart yearned for something more - to reunite with my mom, who had moved to Australia after my high school graduation. I missed her dearly, and after years of being apart, I knew it was time to be with her again.

With Australia as my destination, I bid farewell to Jersey and embarked on a journey that would change my life forever. The land of kangaroos and koalas welcomed me with open arms, and I found myself in awe of the beauty and vastness of the continent. However, challenges awaited me once more, as I had to adapt to a new culture and lifestyle.

Challenges in Australia

Australia was a world away from anything I had experienced before. It was a land of diverse landscapes, from the sandy beaches to the rugged outback. Adjusting to this new environment was both thrilling and overwhelming. The Australian culture was different from what I was accustomed to, and I had to learn to navigate its intricacies.

One of the first challenges I faced was finding a stable job. Although I had experience as a nanny, the job market in Australia proved to be more competitive. However, I was determined to persevere and find a way to support myself.

In the pursuit of stable employment, I also had to confront the feeling of homesickness. Being away from my friends and familiar surroundings in Idaho and Jersey was difficult. I missed the comforting embrace of my family and the cherished memories we had created together.

Love and Conflict

As I settled into life in Australia, I crossed paths with a man who would become a significant figure in my journey. Our connection was instantaneous, and we soon found ourselves drawn to each other.

Since we both had common interests, we connected really quickly. Getting comfortable with him was very easy for me, and I didn't find any difficulty with it. So, it was an easy transition for me.

The End of a Relationship

The decision to part ways was not made lightly, but it was a necessary step towards finding our own paths to happiness. The separation brought a mix of emotions - grief over the end of a significant chapter in my life and a sense of liberation as I embraced newfound independence.

As I navigated the challenges of my life, I reflected on the lessons I had learned throughout my journey. Life had a way of throwing unexpected twists and turns our way, but I had come to realize that these challenges were opportunities for growth and self-discovery.

Finding Strength and Purpose

The trials and triumphs I had experienced in Jersey and Australia had molded me into a stronger and more determined individual. Each obstacle taught me to be adaptable, resilient, and optimistic. The disappointment of not joining the Air Force had transformed into gratitude for the blessing, life had bestowed upon me.

Through it all, I learned the value of self-belief and perseverance. I no longer saw setbacks as failures but as stepping stones towards my true purpose in life. The journey had been arduous, but it had shaped me into the person I was destined to become.

With determination and courage, I was ready to face whatever challenges lay ahead. Life was an unpredictable adventure, and I was eager to embrace each moment with an open heart and a brave spirit.

With a newfound purpose, I knew that I could conquer anything that came my way. Life's unexpected twists have given me the resilience to rise from the ashes and rebuild my life. The journey was far from easy, but it was one filled with growth, love, and the promise of a bright future.

As I moved forward, I held onto the lessons of my past - to be optimistic, to embrace change, and to find strength in the face of adversity. My journey was a testament to the power of perseverance and the beauty of embracing life's uncertainties. As the days turned into weeks and the weeks into months, I found myself settling into a new rhythm of life.

With each passing day, I grew more resilient and self-reliant. The trials I had faced in Jersey and Australia had prepared me for the obstacles I encountered as a single mother. The experiences had taught me to find strength within myself and to trust that I could overcome any hurdle that came my way.

As time went on, I also rekindled my passion for music and movies. I found solace in these artistic expressions, and they became a source of comfort during difficult times. Music was my escape, and it allowed me to connect with my emotions on a deeper level. In moments of reflection, I would lose myself in the lyrics and melodies, finding solace in the harmonies that resonated with my soul.

My love for music grew even bigger when I started following different bands. I discovered that I kind of got connected with the music. It helped me to overcome my negative emotions and allowed me to tune them in a way that helped me to heal from my past traumas and experiences.

This project became a labor of love as I poured my experiences, emotions, and hopes into each song. Through the creative process, I found healing and a renewed sense of purpose.

Through the music, I wanted to inspire others to embrace life's uncertainties and find strength in the face of adversity. I wanted to share my journey of rising from the ashes and rebuilding my life, showing others that they, too, could overcome any challenge that life threw their way.

The trials and triumphs of my journey had taught me that life was unpredictable, but it was also filled with boundless opportunities for growth and self-discovery. Each challenge I faced shaped me into the person I was meant to be, and I wouldn't change a single moment of my past.

I was no longer the young woman who had dreamt of joining the Air Force, nor was I the person who had faced heartbreak in Australia. I was a resilient and empowered woman who had embraced life's twists and turns, transforming challenges into stepping stones towards a brighter future.

In the midst of life's uncertainties, I found my true passion in music. With each passing day, I was grateful for the journey that had led me to this point, knowing that every trial and every triumph had been essential in shaping my path.

As I looked back on my journey, I realized that life didn't always give us happy endings like in the movies. Instead, it presented us with a series of challenges and triumphs that molded us into the individuals we were destined to become. I had come to embrace the rollercoaster of life, knowing that each twist and turn was an opportunity to rise from the ashes and rebuild anew.

And so, my journey continued with an unwavering spirit and a heart filled with gratitude. I knew that life's uncertainties would never end, but I was armed with the resilience and strength to face whatever came my way.

As I continued on my journey, the universe seemed to conspire in my favor, opening doors that I had never imagined possible.

My journey had come full circle - from dreams of joining the Air Force to becoming a strong person. Life's uncertainties had brought me to this point, and I had embraced every twist and turn, finding strength in the face of adversity.

Looking back on my past, I realized that the car accident that had once seemed like a devastating setback had been a catalyst for profound personal growth. It redirected the course of my life, leading me to discover my true passions and purpose. The rejection from the Air Force had been a blessing in disguise, paving the way for a journey of self-discovery and transformation.

As I shared my story with others, I found that my experiences resonated with people from all walks of life. I received messages from individuals who had faced their own challenges and felt inspired by my journey of rising from the ashes. It was a reminder that our stories had the power to connect us, transcending borders and barriers.

Through the highs and lows of life, I learned that happiness was not a destination but a state of mind. It was about finding contentment in the present moment, embracing life's imperfections, and finding beauty in the journey itself.

As I continued to pursue my dreams and advocate for causes close to my heart, I knew that life would continue to surprise me with its twists and turns. But armed with the lessons of resilience and determination, I was ready to face whatever came my way.

And so, my journey of trials and triumphs continued - a testament to the strength of the human spirit and the boundless possibilities that awaited those who dared to dream and persevere. I had risen from the ashes, rebuilt my life, and found my purpose - a journey that I knew would continue to unfold in beautiful and unpredictable ways.

CHAPTER 3

THE UNEXPECTED PREGNANCY

During this chapter of my life, I faced the unexpected challenge of becoming a single mother. It was a significant turning point, and I had to navigate through uncharted waters. The decision to return to my hometown of Idaho was driven by a mix of factors. I despised my time in Australia—it just didn't feel like home, and secondly, I missed my family dearly.

Becoming a nanny was a profession I unexpectedly grew fond of. Strangely enough, as a child, I never liked being around other kids, but as I grew older, they saw me as a mentor, and I embraced this role. Working for a Wall Street family in Jersey, I received affectionate love letters from the kids, particularly one from an eight-year-old boy named George. He even asked me to marry him, and I found it very cute. Despite the initial hesitations, being a nanny turned out to be a fulfilling experience, which eventually led me back to Idaho.

Life took an unexpected turn when I reunited with the person I had the car accident with, Ben. Although it was not a planned reunion, our paths crossed, and emotions from the past resurfaced. However, I made sure to handle the situation maturely and resolved any lingering issues. After some time, I found out that I was pregnant, and this revelation brought its own set of challenges and emotions.

Initially, the biological father of the child wanted me to go for an abortion, but I made the decision to keep the baby. You might wonder how did I end up with the same person with whom I had a car accident. When I returned to my hometown, we decided that we wanted to get into a relationship. At that time, he was stationed in Burton, WA, and would come all the way to Boise to meet me up. We started hanging out with each other at parties and going out and this was the point where we started connecting again. Things escalated between us and I got pregnant. After I received this news, I decided to move back to my father's house to take care of myself.

I was into my 6th month of pregnancy when Ben came and drove me all the way to San Diego. This was not the place that I would get adjusted to. Ben was in Chicago at that time and was married with two girls. Thus, I was not comfortable getting into a relationship with him. He used to send me flowers every day, but I didn't bat an eye on them and would throw them into garbage cans.

Finally, I decided that I wanted to cut ties with this person and never want to see him again since he had already made my life a living hell.

During my pregnancy, I received emotional and little financial support from the father of the child. However, I had already made up my mind about keeping the baby, and I was willing to face whatever challenges lay ahead. Throughout this period, I leaned on my family and friends, seeking their guidance and comfort. Their unwavering support provided me with the strength to embrace motherhood wholeheartedly.

The day my son, Ryan, was born was a mix of emotions. I was excited and anxious, yet ready to embark on this new journey of motherhood. The birth went well, and I was grateful to have my mom and aunt by my side during this momentous occasion.

After my son was born, I made sure that I had minimal contact with his father. Even if there was anything that I wanted help with, I would usually ask my father or Ben's mother to help me with it. Ben's mother openly admitted that she likes me better than her current daughter-in-law.

Becoming a mother transformed me in ways I could never have imagined. I discovered a depth of love and compassion I had never experienced before. My priorities shifted, and I gladly put my children first, even if it meant giving up my corporate aspirations.

While some may view it as sacrificing a career, I saw it as a choice to be there for my kids during their formative years.

Embracing motherhood came with its challenges. I had to learn to balance work and parenting, and there were days when I felt overwhelmed. However, I never allowed these challenges to deter me from being the best mother I could be. I navigated the journey of single motherhood with determination and resilience.

Through it all, I learned valuable life lessons. I understood that life doesn't always go as planned, and sometimes, we have to adapt and make the best of unexpected circumstances. Being a single mother empowered me to be self-reliant, and I discovered a sense of independence that I hadn't known before. I learned to let go of the past and focus on the present, cherishing every moment with my children.

As I reflected on my growth during this chapter of my life, I realized that mistakes were inevitable, but it's how we learn and grow from them that defines us. I embraced my journey as a mother with all its imperfections and embraced the joy that my children brought into my life. Being a mother transformed me into a stronger, more compassionate, and empathetic person. My children became my greatest motivation, and my love for them fueled my determination to provide them with the best life possible.

As I embraced the journey of single motherhood, I soon realized that it was not without its share of challenges. Juggling the responsibilities of being a mother and providing for my family required careful planning and organization. There were days when I felt overwhelmed and exhausted, but the love and joy I experienced from my children made it all worthwhile.

One of the biggest challenges I faced was financial stability. As a single mother, I had to be resourceful and creative in finding ways to make ends meet. I took on odd jobs and freelance work to supplement my income, ensuring that my children had everything they needed. It was a humbling experience, but it also taught me the value of hard work and determination.

Despite the hardships, I remained steadfast in my commitment to being the best mother I could be. I found solace and strength in the support of my family and friends. They were my pillars of strength during times of uncertainty and doubt. Their encouragement and belief in me bolstered my confidence as I navigated through the challenges of single motherhood.

At times, I struggled with feelings of inadequacy. The societal pressure to be a perfect mother weighed heavily on me. I questioned my decisions and worried about whether I was doing enough for my children. However, I learned to silence my doubts and trust my instincts as a mother. Every decision I made was fueled by love and the desire to provide a better life for my kids.

As my children grew older, they became my biggest cheerleaders. Their innocent smiles and laughter brought immense joy to my life. I cherished the moments we spent together, creating memories that would last a lifetime. From picnics in the park to bedtime stories, these simple moments became the highlights of my day.

I realized that motherhood was not about perfection; it was about being present and showing my children unconditional love. They didn't need extravagant gifts or grand gestures. What they needed most was my time and attention. As I embraced this truth, I felt a sense of freedom and liberation from the unrealistic expectations I had placed upon myself.

With time, I began to appreciate the beauty of single motherhood. I reveled in the independence and the sense of accomplishment that came with raising my children on my own. I learned to embrace my identity as a strong, resilient woman and mother. The struggles I faced only made me stronger and more determined to create a better life for my children.

Throughout this journey, I also sought professional guidance to navigate the complexities of single motherhood. I attended parenting workshops and sought counseling to better understand the emotional needs of my children. These resources helped me foster a deeper connection with my kids and provided valuable insights into effective parenting.

As my children continued to grow, I instilled in them the values of compassion, empathy, and resilience. I wanted them to grow up knowing that they could achieve anything they set their minds to. I encouraged their interests and passions, supporting them in every endeavor they pursued.

Being a single mother also taught me the importance of self-care. Amidst the demands of motherhood, I learned that taking care of myself was not selfish but necessary. I made time for hobbies and activities that brought me joy, and I surrounded myself with a supportive network of friends who understood the challenges I faced.

The experience of single motherhood transformed me in ways I had never imagined. It made me more compassionate and understanding of the struggles faced by other parents. I became an advocate for single parents, speaking out about the challenges they faced and advocating for better support systems.

In the midst of unexpected circumstances, I discovered the power of resilience and the strength that lay within me. My journey as a single mother became a testament to the human spirit's ability to endure and overcome adversity. I realized that life's challenges were not meant to break us but to shape us into stronger, more compassionate individuals.

As my children grew older, they became my partners in this journey of life. We faced every hurdle together, celebrating each triumph and supporting one another through difficult times. My bond with my children deepened, and I felt a profound sense of pride in the remarkable individuals they were becoming.

The unexpected pregnancy and the birth of my son, Ryan, not only shaped my future plans and aspirations but also taught me the true meaning of unconditional love. As a single mother, I learned to let go of societal expectations and embrace my unique path in life. I discovered that being a mother was not defined by marital status, but by the love and devotion, I poured into my children.

Looking back, I wouldn't change a single moment of my journey as a single mother. It was a chapter filled with ups and downs, joys and sorrows, but above all, it was a chapter of growth and transformation. I found strength in vulnerability, and I discovered my purpose in the love I shared with my children.

As I continue on this journey of motherhood, I hold onto the lessons I've learned and the memories we've created. My children are my greatest blessings, and I am eternally grateful for the privilege of being their mother. They have taught me the true meaning of love and have given my life a sense of purpose and fulfillment that I could have never imagined.

As the years passed, my children continued to grow and blossom into remarkable individuals. Each day brought new adventures and cherished memories that added richness to the tapestry of our lives. Despite the challenges that life threw our way, we faced them as a united front, relying on the strength of our bond and the love that bound us together.

As a single mother, I strived to provide a stable and nurturing environment for my children. I worked diligently to instill in them the values of resilience, kindness, and compassion. We faced financial constraints at times, but we learned to make the most of what we had and found joy in simple pleasures.

In the midst of my responsibilities as a mother, I also embarked on a journey of self-discovery. I delved into my passions and interests, finding solace and rejuvenation in creative pursuits. I learned that taking care of myself was not only essential for my well-being but also set an example for my children to prioritize self-care.

One of the most significant challenges I encountered during this time was finding a balance between being a mother and pursuing my own dreams. I grappled with feelings of guilt, wondering if I was dedicating enough time and attention to my children. However, I came to realize that pursuing my passions didn't diminish my role as a mother; rather, it made me a happier and more fulfilled person, which ultimately benefited my children.

Despite the challenges of single motherhood, I never lost sight of my dreams and aspirations. I found inspiration in my children, who looked up to me as a role model of strength and resilience. Their belief in me pushed me to push myself further and reach new heights.

In the professional realm, I sought opportunities that aligned with my passions and values. I began writing and sharing my experiences as a single mother, hoping to inspire and empower others who walked a similar path. Through my words, I aimed to break the stigma surrounding single parenthood and shed light on the incredible strength and determination exhibited by single mothers worldwide.

During this time, I also reconnected with old friends and made new ones who became an integral part of my support system. We shared laughter, tears, and triumphs, standing by each other through life's ups and downs. These friendships enriched my life and reinforced the importance of community and solidarity.

As my children grew older, they began to understand the unique circumstances of our family. We openly discussed the challenges we faced and the lessons we learned. I wanted them to know that life wasn't always a smooth ride, but it was essential to navigate the rough waters with grace and resilience.

Motherhood taught me the art of adaptability. I learned to be flexible and embrace change, knowing that life's twists and turns were opportunities for growth. It was through these experiences that I learned to embrace uncertainty and trust that things would work out in the end.

The bond between my children and me deepened with time. We shared laughter, tears, and heart-to-heart conversations that strengthened our connection. I was grateful for their openness and willingness to share their feelings with me, which allowed me to better understand their needs and aspirations.

In the pursuit of my own dreams, I found success as an author, sharing my experiences and insights through books and articles. My writing became a platform to advocate for single mothers and empower them to embrace their strength and resilience. I received countless messages from women worldwide, thanking me for being a voice that resonated with their own experiences.

As my journey as a single mother continued, I couldn't help but marvel at the beautiful tapestry of life that had unfolded. It was a tapestry woven with love, challenges, growth, and triumphs—a tapestry that showcased the incredible strength of the human spirit.

As I look back on the chapters of my life, each one uniquely shaped my identity and molded me into the woman I am today. From the dreams of joining the Air Force to the unexpected pregnancy and the joys and challenges of single motherhood, every experience contributed to the person I had become.

As I continue to embrace each new chapter with courage and determination, I am grateful for the blessings life has bestowed upon me. My journey as a single mother has taught me the true meaning of love, resilience, and perseverance. I have learned that life's obstacles are not roadblocks but opportunities for growth and transformation.

Through it all, I stand tall and proud, a single mother who has found her voice and purpose in this vast world. I am a mother, a writer, an advocate, and a woman who believes in the power of love and the strength of the human spirit. My story is one of hope and inspiration, a testament to the extraordinary possibilities that await those who dare to dream and embrace life's journey with an open heart.

As I pen the final lines of this chapter, I am filled with a sense of gratitude for the blessings that have graced my life—the love of my children, the unwavering support of family and friends, and the fulfillment that comes from living life authentically.

To all the single mothers out there, know that you are not alone. Your journey may be challenging, but it is also filled with boundless love and joy. Embrace every moment, celebrate your victories, and never forget the incredible power that resides within you.

And so, as the sun sets on this chapter of my life, I eagerly await the dawn of a new one. I am excited for the adventures that lie ahead, the lessons waiting to be learned, and the love that will continue to shape my journey.

With a heart full of gratitude and a spirit brimming with hope, I welcome the next chapter with open arms. For in the tapestry of life, there is always another thread to be woven, another story to be told, and another chapter to be lived.

Part 2

The Calamity

CHAPTER 4

THE LOVE OF HER LIFE

As I reflect on the moment I first met Travis, it feels like it happened just yesterday. I had recently moved to Lemhi County, Idaho, and a common friend introduced me to Travis at a party. From the very beginning, there was an instant connection between us. Travis was a true gentleman, and his charm and sense of humor were simply irresistible. Even though I annoyed him with my quirky ways, he still tolerated me with grace, and that left me intrigued. It was almost as if our souls recognized each other, and we just clicked.

As we spent more time together, I couldn't help but notice the qualities in Travis that stood out and convinced me he was the one for me. He was genuine, loving, and compassionate. He had an old-fashioned charm that appealed to me, and his ability to make me laugh even on my darkest days was truly magical. Unlike the relationships I had experienced before, being with Travis felt effortless. It wasn't a struggle; it was a natural flow of love and understanding.

Our love story began with a sense of serendipity as if the universe conspired to bring us together. Sitting in that restaurant, Travis surprised me with a spontaneous invitation to a trip to the West Coast. His whimsical nature was endearing, and I couldn't help but be drawn to his adventurous spirit. We embarked on that journey together, and little did I know it was just the beginning of a beautiful chapter in my life.

As our relationship blossomed, it became evident that Travis and I shared the same ideals and dreams. Our bond grew stronger with each passing day, and we found comfort in knowing that we were on the same page about our future. Travis supported my aspirations, just as I supported his passion for river rafting. He encouraged me to embrace new experiences, to live life to the fullest, and to never shy away from adventure.

Travis's enthusiasm for life was infectious, and it opened my eyes to a world of possibilities. Together, we discovered the joy of exploring nature, seeking thrilling experiences, and cherishing every moment we spent together. His presence brought a sense of security and comfort that I had never known before. I knew deep within my heart that he was the one I wanted to share my life with.

The journey of blending our families was both heartwarming and challenging. Travis's loving and nurturing nature made it easier for my children to embrace him as a father figure. When they heard the devastating news of his passing, they rushed to the ranch to grieve together. Ryan, my son, was particularly affected, and his pain found an outlet in punching a dent in a pickup truck. Despite his emotions, Travis had always been patient with my children, understanding the complexities of blending a family.

Travis's interactions with my children were a source of immense joy for me. He connected with them on a deep level, becoming a mentor and a role model they could look up to. His kindness and sweetness were evident in every interaction, and he took the time to educate and guide them. Travis contributed to their growth and well-being, leaving a lasting impact on their lives.

During our journey as a blended family, we had our share of challenges. I'll admit my passionate nature sometimes led to disagreements, but Travis's calming presence and ability to ignore my rants diffused tension and brought harmony to our home. He had the rare ability to navigate through tough situations with grace, and his unwavering love for us made the difficult moments easier to overcome.

Finding love with Travis was truly a second chance for me. My previous experiences had taught me valuable lessons, and I knew that I deserved something bigger and better. When he came into my life, it felt like a rescue mission. He saved me from a life of turmoil and sadness, and with him, I found the happiness and love that had eluded me before.

Our love story became a beacon of hope for those facing difficult circumstances. It showcased the power of second chances and the transformative nature of love. I firmly believe that happiness can be found when we open ourselves to the possibility of love and embrace the people who come into our lives.

Our decision to marry each other was not driven by external pressures or societal norms. It was an expression of our genuine love for one another. We didn't have an extravagant wedding; instead, we opted for a simple courthouse ceremony. We were both in the midst of divorces from our previous partners, and life had thrown us into unexpected situations. Nevertheless, we decided to make our union official and embark on this new journey together.

On the day of our courthouse wedding, we stood in front of the judge in casual clothes, and there was an air of lightheartedness around us. The judge looked at me, then at Travis, and then back at me as if to confirm if I was sure about this decision. I couldn't help but chuckle, and we both reassured the judge that we were absolutely certain about getting married. It was a moment of joy and laughter, and it felt like the universe was conspiring to bring us together.

After our marriage, we didn't go on a traditional honeymoon, but it didn't matter to us. Our love and connection were more meaningful than any extravagant trip. We celebrated our union by opening a bottle of champagne and cherishing the special moments together. However, an unfortunate turn of events marred what was supposed to be a joyous occasion. My ex-boyfriend attempted to sabotage our wedding plans, leading to the abrupt cancellation of the event. But in the end, it turned out to be a blessing in disguise, as it further solidified our commitment to each other.

Soon after our marriage, we were filled with excitement and hope as we attempted to start a family. However, we faced the heartbreak of a miscarriage. It was a painful experience for both of us, and we mourned the loss of the little life that had started to grow inside me. But we didn't lose hope, and our perseverance paid off when we found out we were expecting again in September.

This time, I was cautious and protective of our unborn child. I kept the news to myself until I was certain that Christopher was safe and healthy. I even hid it from my family and friends, and on certain occasions, whenever they offered me to drink, I would deny and they all though that I was a weirdo. I would usually sneak out, make a mixed drink, which was more like tonic water, and pretend that I was drinking. In March, we joyfully announced the pregnancy to our family and friends, and the anticipation of becoming parents filled our hearts with happiness and nervousness.

The journey of bringing Christopher into this world was far from easy. I knew that giving birth in my 30s could pose challenges, especially in a rural hospital, and I was certain that I would die very soon. The fear of the unknown weighed on me, but I was determined to face it head-on. During the delivery, I was administered roofie fentanyl to ease the pain, but it caused me to pass out momentarily. Travis was by my side, waking me up and encouraging me to push through the pain.

In those intense moments, I gathered every ounce of strength within me, and with the support of Travis and the medical team, I pushed Christopher into this world. It was a moment of triumph and exhaustion as the tiny 5-pound bundle of joy was placed on my lap. Travis and Christopher's bond was instant, and they became inseparable. I admit it took me a little longer to form that deep connection with my lion cub, as I lovingly called him, but as the days went by, my heart embraced him completely.

As we settled into our roles as parents, our lives transformed in beautiful ways. Travis and Christopher became the center of my universe, and I found a newfound purpose in nurturing and caring for them. Our little family of three was a source of endless joy, laughter, and love. As we embarked on this journey together, I knew that Travis was indeed the love of my life, and I was grateful for every moment we shared.

As the days turned into weeks and weeks into months, our bond as a family grew stronger. Travis, Christopher, and I created our own little world filled with love and laughter. Every milestone that Christopher achieved, from his first smile to his first steps, brought us immeasurable joy. We celebrated each victory as a family, cherishing the precious moments that made our hearts swell with pride.

Travis, being an adventurous soul, introduced me to the thrill of river rafting. It was one of his passions, and he wanted to share the experience with me. I'll admit I was initially hesitant about going on a river rafting trip. The idea of navigating through rushing waters and rapids made me nervous, but Travis assured me that he would be there to guide and protect me.

Finally, I decided to give it a try, and we planned our fateful river rafting trip. It was a beautiful day, and the sun-kissed the surface of the water, creating a mesmerizing dance of light and shadows. As we set off on our rafting adventure, a mix of excitement and apprehension coursed through my veins.

The initial part of the trip was thrilling yet manageable. Travis skillfully maneuvered the raft, and I felt a surge of adrenaline as we glided through the water. My initial reservations started to fade away as I began to enjoy the experience. Travis's reassuring presence gave me a sense of security, and I started to embrace the excitement of the adventure.

As we continued our journey down the river, the worries and stress of everyday life seemed to melt away. The breathtaking scenery surrounded us, and the rush of the river filled our ears, drowning out any lingering doubts. Travis's infectious laughter echoed through the canyon walls, and I couldn't help but join in, feeling an unbridled sense of joy in his company.

The river seemed to have a life of its own, twisting and turning as if leading us on an enchanting dance. Travis navigated the rapids with ease, and I marveled at his skill and passion for this exhilarating sport. With each passing moment, my trust in him deepened, and I felt a newfound appreciation for the adventures he had introduced me to.

We stopped along the riverbank for a picnic, laughing and sharing stories as we basked in the warm sunlight. I watched as Travis interacted with my children, his playful and caring nature shining through. It warmed my heart to see the bond he had formed with them and how seamlessly he had become a part of our family.

As the day drew to a close, the sky painted a breathtaking canvas of colors. The sun began its descent, casting a golden glow on the water. We drifted slowly, savoring every precious moment of togetherness. It was in these moments of tranquility that I felt a profound sense of gratitude for the life I had built with Travis.

With him by my side, I felt like I could conquer anything that life threw my way. He was my rock, my anchor, and I knew that no matter what challenges we faced, we would face them together. The journey we had embarked on that day was not just a river rafting trip; it was a testament to the strength of our love and the resilience of our bond.

As we returned to our daily lives, the memories of that fateful river rafting trip stayed with me like a cherished keepsake. I would often find myself drifting back to that day, reliving the moments of joy, laughter, and love we had shared. It had been a turning point in our relationship, strengthening our connection and deepening our commitment to each other.

Travis continued to pursue his passion for river rafting, and I eagerly joined him on many more adventures. Each trip brought new challenges and triumphs, and together, we navigated the untamed waters of life. I had discovered a side of myself that I never knew existed, embracing the thrill of adventure and the beauty of nature.

Through our shared experiences, we grew as individuals and as a couple. We supported each other's dreams and aspirations, celebrating each other's victories and providing a shoulder to lean on during moments of setbacks. Travis's adventurous spirit inspired me to step out of my comfort zone and explore the world with an open heart and a curious mind.

Our love continued to blossom, and with each passing day, I fell more deeply in love with the man who had not only captured my heart but had also become my partner in life's grand adventure. We faced challenges together, weathered storms hand in hand and rejoiced in the simple pleasures of life. Our love was a beacon of hope, guiding us through the highs and lows of life's unpredictable journey.

As the years passed, we created a lifetime of cherished memories, from the joyous laughter of our children to the quiet moments of reflection by the river. Travis's love had transformed my life in ways I could never have imagined, and I was grateful for every twist and turn that led us to this beautiful chapter of our story.

Our fateful river rafting trip had marked the beginning of a new chapter in our lives—a chapter filled with love, adventure, and the unbreakable bond we shared. It was a chapter that I would forever hold dear to my heart, a testament to the power of love to heal, inspire, and carry us through life's most challenging waters.

As I looked back on that day, I couldn't help but smile at the serendipity of it all. What had started as a hesitant step into the unknown had turned into a journey of a lifetime—a journey that I was grateful to share with the love of my life, Travis. With him, I had found the courage to embrace life's adventures and to savor every precious moment, knowing that love would always light the way.

And so, as I closed this chapter of our story, I looked ahead with hope and excitement for the chapters yet to come. I knew that our love would continue to guide us, anchoring us in times of turmoil and lifting us to new heights of joy and happiness. With Travis by my side, I was ready to embrace whatever the future held, knowing that our love would be the constant thread woven through the tapestry of our lives.

As the sun dipped below the horizon, casting a warm glow over the world, I took one last glance at the river that had been the backdrop of our fateful journey. It was a reminder of the beauty and unpredictability of life, and I knew that I was ready to face whatever lay ahead, hand in hand with the love of my life, my partner in adventure, and my anchor in the storm. Together, we would navigate the rivers of life, knowing that our love was the compass that would always lead us home.

CHAPTER 5

THE FATEFUL RAFTING TRIP

I was scared, my heart pounding loudly in my chest as I prepared for the river rafting trip. My intuition was whispering warnings to me, urging me to reconsider this adventure. But there was Travis, beaming with excitement and determination, his eyes filled with the thrill of adventure. He had been looking forward to this trip for so long, and I couldn't bear to dampen his enthusiasm.

As much as I wanted to trust Travis's judgment, my reservations gnawed at me. I tried to convince him to cancel the trip, telling him that we could do something else together, something safer. But he was adamant, assuring me that everything would be fine and that he had taken all the necessary precautions.

"I promise, Rebecca, we'll be careful, and it's going to be an amazing experience," he said with his trademark charming smile.

Reluctantly, I agreed to go along with the plan, suppressing the unease churning in my stomach. I called my mom for some reassurance, hoping she would support my decision to cancel. However, she surprised me with her understanding and simple advice, "Just say if you don't wanna go." But my love for Travis and my desire not to disappoint him kept me from speaking my true feelings.

The morning of the trip, we gathered all our gear, packed a picnic, and started preparing for the rafting trip. Travis had left the raft at his parents' place, so he traveled a forty-mile journey to retrieve it.

With the raft in tow, Travis came and picked me up, and we made our way to the river, where our adventure awaited. As we unloaded the raft and prepared ourselves, I watched Travis with a mix of admiration and apprehension. He had such a passion for river rafting, and his expertise was evident as he meticulously checked every detail.

"Are you sure about this, Travis?" I asked one last time.

"I've done this countless times, and it's always been fantastic. Don't worry; I've got it all under control," he reassured me, giving my hand a reassuring squeeze.

With a deep breath, I decided to trust him, hoping that my intuition was wrong and that this would indeed be a fantastic experience. We pushed the raft into the water and hopped in, our journey on the river beginning.

At first, the waters were calm and serene, almost hypnotic in their tranquility. Travis skillfully navigated the raft, guiding us through the gentle currents. The scenery around us was breathtaking, and I started to relax, allowing myself to get lost in the beauty of nature.

As we continued our journey in the river, the boat abruptly flipped in the water, and we found ourselves submerged in the icy embrace of the river. Panic grips my heart as I fight to resurface, disoriented and struggling against the strong current. The world around me blurs into a chaotic blur of water and shadows.

Travis, Christopher, and I were separated in the chaos. My heart pounded in my chest as I desperately tried to find them in the swirling waters. The fear of losing them was overwhelming, and I fought against the current with all my strength. The sound of rushing water echoed in my ears as I called out their names, hoping they could hear me above the roar.

As I fought to stay afloat, memories of our time together flashed before my eyes. The laughter, the love, and the moments we shared became a lifeline that kept me going. I couldn't give up; I had to find Travis and Christopher. They were my anchor, my reason to keep pushing forward.

Desperately, I try to find Travis, my arms flailing in the water, searching for his familiar touch. My lungs ache for air as I continue to fight against the rushing current. Fear grips me, and all I can think about is the safety of my husband.

I couldn't help but replay the events of the day in my mind. We had set out on that river rafting trip filled with excitement and joy, looking forward to creating more beautiful memories together as a family. Travis, with his passion for adventure, had been eager to share his love for rafting with us, and Christopher was thrilled to be part of the journey.

However, our dreams of a perfect day were shattered when the river's currents grew wild and unpredictable. In a split second, our raft hit a treacherous rapid, throwing us all into the cold, turbulent waters. I struggled to stay afloat, my body slammed against rocks and debris as I desperately searched for Travis and Christopher. But they were nowhere to be seen.

Finally, my survival instincts kicked in, and I grabbed the rope of the boat and tried to get on the surface of the river. Luckily, I got hold of the ranch on the little island and pulled myself up. I scrutinized the area in hopes of finding Travis and Christopher, but all I could see was our boat floating upside down. My heart clenches in terror as I call out his name, the water swallowing my desperate cries. Where is he? What happened to him?

Fearful and disoriented, I cling to it for dear life, praying that Travis will emerge from the water any moment. But as the seconds tick by, hope wanes, and a sense of dread settles in my gut.

Suddenly, I catch a glimpse of something in the water downstream. It's Travis holding Christopher above his head, trying to save him from the water. Upon closer look, I noticed that Travis's head was gushing with blood, and he was not conscious. He hit a rock in the river when the boat flipped.

The night air was chilling, and I shivered uncontrollably as I stood on the riverbank, still in shock from the tragedy that had unfolded before my eyes. The sound of rushing water seemed to echo the chaos within my mind, and I felt like I was drowning in grief and disbelief.

Finally, as the night wore on, the search and rescue team made a heartbreaking discovery. Travis and Christopher's lifeless bodies were found tangled amidst the rocks and branches in the river. The world around me seemed to come to a standstill as I stared at the lifeless forms of the two people I loved most.

At that moment, my heart shattered into a million pieces. The pain was overwhelming, and I couldn't fathom how I would ever go on without them. They were my world, my everything, and now they were gone, leaving behind a void that could never be filled.

The days that followed were a blur of grief and mourning. The weight of the loss was suffocating, and I found it hard to breathe without them by my side. I leaned on friends and family for support, but the pain was indescribable, and no words of comfort could ease my suffering.

As I was pulled out of the water, my body felt numb, and my mind was filled with a mix of emotions – sorrow, anger, and disbelief. I clung to the hope that this was all just a horrible nightmare, that I would wake up and find Travis and Christopher safe and sound.

But as the cold air hit my wet skin, reality crashed down on me once again. They were gone, and I was left to navigate a world without them. The journey ahead seemed daunting, but I knew that I had to find the strength to carry on for the sake of Christopher.

As the local search and rescue team arrived, a wave of relief washed over me, but it was quickly replaced by a sense of overwhelming grief. Travis and Christopher were gone, and the river had taken them from me. The darkness of the night seemed to mirror the darkness that now filled my heart.

With tear-filled eyes, I watched as the rescue team retrieved Travis's lifeless body from the water. His head was gushing with blood, a haunting image that would forever be etched in my memory. I couldn't bear to look, but I couldn't tear my gaze away either.

The paramedics worked tirelessly to save Christopher, but it was too late. His heart was barely beating when they got to him, and despite their best efforts, they couldn't bring him back to life. My precious son was gone, leaving a void in my life that could never be filled.

As they loaded us onto an ambulance for transportation to the hospital, I clung to the hope that somehow, miraculously, Travis and Christopher would be okay. But deep down, I knew that they were gone, taken from me in a tragic accident that would forever change the course of my life.

In the hospital, the reality of the situation hit me like a ton of bricks. Travis and Christopher were gone, and I was left to navigate a world without them. The pain was unbearable, and I felt like I was drowning in a sea of grief.

Over the next few days, friends and family gathered around me, offering their love and support, but nothing could ease the pain of losing the two most important people in my life. The house that once echoed with laughter and joy now felt empty and cold.

In the quiet moments, I found myself replaying the events of that fateful day in my mind. I blamed myself for not convincing Travis to cancel the rafting trip, for not being more insistent when my intuition screamed that something bad would happen.

The accident had shattered my world, leaving me lost and broken. Travis had been my rock, my partner in life, and Christopher had been my ray of sunshine, bringing joy and laughter to every moment. Without them, I felt like I was drifting aimlessly, trying to make sense of a life that no longer made sense.

In the face of such a devastating loss, I struggled to find the strength to move forward. But somewhere deep within me, I knew that Travis and Christopher would want me to keep going, to find a way to honor their memory and live my life to the fullest.

As I slowly began to rebuild my life, I leaned on the love and support of those around me. The pain of their absence would never fully go away, but I found solace in the memories we had shared and the love we had for each other.

I knew that Travis and Christopher would want me to find happiness again, to embrace life with the same sense of adventure and joy that they had. They had been taken from me too soon, but their love would forever live on in my heart.

The river rafting trip that was meant to be an exciting adventure had turned into a heartbreaking tragedy, and it would take me a lifetime to come to terms with the loss of Travis and Christopher. But I vowed to carry their memory with me every step of the way, to find strength in their love, and to honor them by living a life filled with love, courage, and gratitude.

As I move forward, I know that there will be moments of darkness and despair, but I will also find moments of light and hope. I will cherish the memories of the love we shared and find comfort in knowing that Travis and Christopher will always be with me, guiding me through life's journey, even in their absence.

And so, I face an uncertain future, one that I never could have imagined or prepared for. But I will carry the love of Travis and Christopher in my heart, and with each new day, I will take a step forward, navigating this life without them but never forgetting the impact they had on my life and the love we shared.

The hospital waiting room was filled with sorrow, and the social worker approached me with a heavy heart. She had known my dad, a well-connected politician, and her eyes were bloodshot from tears as she tried to find the right words to comfort me. Another girl, Jamie, was there with me, providing support during this unimaginable ordeal.

It seemed like everyone around me already knew the devastating news, which was later confirmed by the doctor when he arrived to face me with the heartbreaking truth. Christopher was gone. My little ray of sunshine, my precious son, had passed away. I looked at the clock, and it felt like time had stopped in that moment of anguish.

When the doctor asked if I wanted to see Christopher, I was overwhelmed with conflicting emotions. Anger and denial surged within me, and I couldn't bear the thought of seeing my lifeless child. Jamie, ever the protector, piped up, suggesting that I should see him. But I couldn't comprehend the idea of facing that reality. I refused.

In the aftermath of the tragedy, I was admitted to the ICU, where the medical team monitored me closely. They were concerned about my physical health, but it was my heart that had been shattered into a million pieces. The pain of losing my husband and child was unbearable, and I was in shock.

My sister Jennifer stayed by my side throughout this ordeal, supporting me in any way she could. I sought comfort in her presence, but the magnitude of the loss had created a chasm between us. We both struggled to cope with the grief, and our relationship felt strained.

As days turned into weeks, I tried to find a semblance of normalcy, but the pain was always there, gnawing at my soul. I moved with Jennifer in Bosie after the incident, and we shared a heart-wrenching moment when I asked her what Christopher looked like when she saw him. She said he looked peaceful, and we clung to each other, sobbing. But amidst the sorrow, anger reared its head again.

I couldn't fathom why Jennifer had chosen to see Christopher, why she subjected herself to that heartache. I wanted to protect her from the pain, but she explained that it was her way of finding closure. My emotions were tumultuous, and although I understood her need for closure, I couldn't help but feel anger at her for having that last image of my son in her head.

In the wake of the tragedy, I faced not only the grief of losing my family but also the complexities of navigating relationships. My family and friends were there, but their attention was often directed towards my sister as if my grief was secondary. It hurt to see my pain overshadowed, but I also understood that grief can be a complicated journey for everyone involved.

As days turned into weeks, I tried to cope with the pain and loss on my own terms. I found myself isolated in my grief, feeling like an afterthought in my own tragedy. It was a lonely and dark place, and I struggled to find solace in the support offered by others.

My relationship with Jennifer had changed, and it was difficult to find the connection we once had. We both coped with grief in different ways, and it created a void between us. I wanted to reach out to bridge the gap between us, but it felt like an impossible task.

In the midst of this turmoil, I tried to find ways to honor the memory of Travis and Christopher. I held onto the love we shared, cherishing the precious moments we had together. I knew they would want me to find happiness again, to continue living, but the pain was relentless.

Grief is a complex journey, and it took time for me to realize that everyone copes differently. My family and friends may not have fully understood the depth of my pain, but they were grappling with their own emotions, too. I had to find a way to communicate my feelings and needs, to let them know that I needed their support and love.

It was a difficult road, but slowly, I started to open up to those around me. I shared my pain and vulnerability, allowing myself to be seen in my darkest moments. And as I did, I began to see glimpses of understanding and empathy from my loved ones.

With time, I also learned to be patient with myself. Grieving is not a linear process, and there is no timeline for healing. I had to allow myself to feel the pain, to honor the love I had for Travis and Christopher, and to find my way through the darkness.

In the midst of my grief, I found moments of clarity and hope. I saw the true colors of my family and friends, realizing that while they may not have fully grasped the magnitude of my pain, they still cared for me in their own way. It was a humbling and eye-opening experience.

As the days turned into months, I continued to grapple with grief and relationships. It was a rollercoaster of emotions, but through it all, I held onto the love that Travis and Christopher had brought into my life.

I knew that their memory would forever be a part of me, guiding me through life's ups and downs. They were my heart and soul, and even in their absence, their love continued to shape the person I was becoming.

And so, I navigated the treacherous waters of grief and relationships, seeking healing and understanding along the way. I learned to lean on those who offered support, to communicate my needs, and to find solace in the cherished memories of the family I had lost.

In the midst of tragedy, I found strength in embracing my vulnerability and allowing myself to be seen and heard. It was a painful and transformative journey, but one that led me to a place of acceptance and growth.

As I continued to move forward, I knew that the road ahead would be challenging, but I also knew that I had the love and support of those who cared for me. I would honor the memory of Travis and Christopher by living a life filled with love, resilience, and gratitude.

Grief would forever be a part of me, but it would not define me. I was a survivor, a testament to the enduring power of love, and I would carry the legacy of my family in my heart forever and always.

As I attempted to heal from the loss of Travis and Christopher, I faced another challenge that stemmed from the tragedy – my fear of water. Water had become a reminder of the heart-wrenching accident that took away my beloved husband and son. Even the kids, who once loved rafting, now refused to engage in any water activities. The wounds were still fresh, and it was difficult for all of us to confront the fear and pain associated with the river.

I understood that healing takes time and that each person copes differently. For now, I respected my children's and my own boundaries when it came to water-related activities. We allowed ourselves to grieve and process the trauma at our own pace, supporting each other through the process.

In the aftermath of the tragic loss of Travis and Christopher, counseling became a topic of discussion. Many well-meaning individuals suggested it as a way to help me navigate the overwhelming grief, but I was hesitant to seek professional help. I had a strong support system of friends and family, including Rob, who is like a big brother and became a pillar of strength for me. He checked on me daily, ensuring I was taking care of myself and offering his unwavering support. He was always there when I needed him.

Despite having a robust support system, there were external factors that led me to take counseling. The traumatic experience of being physically assaulted by someone and then being falsely accused of being the perpetrator forced me into therapy. The court ordered me to undergo counseling, which left me feeling unjustly burdened. The therapist was puzzled about why I was there, as my situation had nothing to do with the loss of Travis and Christopher. I expressed my frustration at being wrongly sent to therapy, and I left the therapy session after a quarrel with my therapist.

Grief is a journey with no set path, and the process of healing is unique to each individual. I recognized that counseling, while helpful for some, might not be the answer for everyone. For me, the support of my friends and family was an essential aspect of healing and moving forward.

In time, I found ways to cope with the pain, and I allowed myself to experience the emotions that came with grief. I embraced vulnerability and found strength in the love and memories shared with Travis and Christopher. Their legacies became a driving force, motivating me to live life fully despite the heartache.

Although the pain of their loss will always be a part of me, I learned that it's possible to find joy and happiness amid grief. By surrounding myself with understanding and compassionate people, I discovered the power of resilience and the human spirit's ability to endure and thrive.

Life is a tapestry woven with both joy and sorrow, and my journey has taught me to appreciate every moment. I am grateful for the support of my loved ones, the memories that bring me comfort, and the knowledge that, even in the darkest of times, there is light to guide me forward.

So, as I continue on this path of healing and growth, I am determined to honor the memory of Travis and Christopher by living life to the fullest, embracing both the joys and the challenges that come my way. Their love remains an eternal flame in my heart, guiding me through the waters of life, helping me navigate the currents of grief, and inspiring me to find solace and strength in every dawn that breaks through the darkness.

CHAPTER 6
DESPERATE MOMENTS

As I navigated through the storm of emotions that followed the tragic loss of Travis and Christopher, I found myself drowning in a sea of despair. Every day felt like a battle, and I struggled to find the strength to carry on. The weight of grief pressed down on me, and I wondered if I would ever see the light again.

I hated everyone and everything around me, feeling an overwhelming sense of emptiness that seemed impossible to fill. To cope, I tried to throw myself into various activities, attempting to fill the void left by their absence. But the misery that clung to me sought solace in the company of others, a selfish act to shift the burden from my shoulders. It was a stage, I knew, but one that threatened to consume me entirely.

The tragedy had shaken my faith, leaving me questioning the existence of any higher power. I grappled with the idea of religion, once anti-religious, now lost in the vast expanse of uncertainty. The pain was all-consuming, and I struggled to find a way out of the darkness.

Time blurred as days turned into weeks, and I found myself immersed in entrepreneurship. I founded a construction company called Titan Construction, seeking solace in hard work and tireless dedication. While it kept me busy, it was also a way to avoid confronting my grief directly. The company is not in operation now, but I found myself immersed in Titan Productions, where I produced films and music. It was a relentless journey, working around the clock, traveling, and meeting people.

Finding closure amidst overwhelming grief proved to be an elusive task. Waves of emotions crashed over me, and I felt adrift in the sea of despair. There were moments when I felt a glimmer of hope, but they were fleeting, lost amid the overwhelming pain. I yearned to find myself again, to rediscover the person I once was before the calamity struck.

Amidst the struggles, memories of happy moments with Travis and Christopher both comforted and pained me. One of the most prominent memories was a camping trip where I watched Travis teach our children how to build a fire. He was patient, kind, and passionate, a gentle teacher guiding them through life's lessons. It was a beautiful memory, but it only amplified the ache of their absence.

The impact of losing their father and brother was immense on Ryan and Emma, sending ripples of grief through their young lives. As their mother, I witnessed their pain and struggles up close, and it tore at my heart to see them suffer.

Ryan, my son, grappled with overwhelming anger. His emotions were a tempest, and he often lashed out at the world around him in a desperate attempt to cope with his pain. His grief manifested itself in bursts of frustration and rage, leaving him feeling lost and confused. I did my best to comfort him, but it was clear that his wounds ran deep.

One day, in a moment of intense emotion, Ryan unleashed his fury on his grandmother's new car, smashing it in an outpouring of pent-up grief. The sight of him venting his pain through such destructive means broke my heart even further, and I knew that he needed support and understanding to heal.

Emma, my daughter, was quieter in her grief, internalizing her pain and occasionally letting it out in bursts. She struggled to process her emotions, and her heartache weighed heavily on her young shoulders. It was heartrending to witness her vulnerability, and I wanted nothing more than to ease her pain.

To shield my children from my own despair, I tried to create a facade of strength and resilience. I didn't want them to see me crumble under the weight of grief, fearing it would only amplify their own struggles. It was a delicate balance, wanting to be a source of comfort for them while struggling to find comfort myself.

Through it all, I encouraged Ryan and Emma to express their feelings openly and honestly. I wanted them to know that their emotions were valid and that there was no right or wrong way to grieve. Whenever they needed to let it out, I urged them not to hold back. If Ryan wanted to break something, I told him it was okay to let it out and get it out of his system. Emma, on the other hand, would sometimes let her tears flow, and I assured her that it was alright to cry.

In the face of such profound loss, I tried my best to instill a sense of courage and fearlessness in my children. I wanted them to know that it was okay to feel scared and vulnerable but also that they had the strength to face their pain and grow from it. Life had dealt them an unimaginable blow, but I believed in their resilience and knew that they could find their way through the darkness.

As I journeyed through my own healing process, I remained committed to supporting Ryan and Emma in theirs. We may have been wounded, but we were also bound by love and a shared determination to honor the memory of their father and brother.

No, I didn't attend any counseling sessions despite the suggestion that it might be helpful for me. While I recognized the value of professional guidance and support, I found it difficult to open up to strangers about my innermost struggles. The idea of pouring my heart out to someone I didn't know felt intimidating and uncomfortable.

As I sat in that counseling room, the weight of my grief pressing down on my chest, I yearned for someone to understand and help me navigate the turbulent waters of my emotions. But as the counselor began speaking, there was an underlying tone of dismissiveness and impatience in their words that cut through me like a knife. It felt as though they were judging me for my silence, making me feel small and insignificant.

My vulnerability was met with callousness, and the walls around me grew taller and thicker. I couldn't bring myself to open up to someone who seemed uninterested in truly understanding my pain. The counselor's lack of empathy left me feeling even more alone and isolated. Instead of finding solace in counseling, I discovered my own way of coping with the immense loss. I chose to share my emotions in a different manner - through helping others. It became a cathartic outlet for me to extend a hand to those who were also grappling with their own hardships. Whether it was lending a listening ear or offering support, being there for others brought a sense of purpose and healing to my own wounded heart.

As I reached out to others, I realized that sharing my experiences not only allowed me to connect with them on a deeper level but also brought a sense of comfort to those going through similar struggles. It was as if my pain had a purpose, and by channeling it into support for others, I found a way to make sense of the tragedy that had befallen my life.

In my interactions with others, I didn't pretend to have all the answers or present myself as a flawless role model. I was just a woman, a mother, trying to navigate the turbulent waters of grief while extending a hand to others in need. It wasn't about portraying myself as invincible; instead, it was about acknowledging our shared vulnerability and embracing the healing power of human connection.

People often wonder why I invest so much energy into helping others, even while carrying the weight of my own pain. The truth is, seeing a smile on someone's face and witnessing the spark of hope reignite in their eyes brings a sense of fulfillment that I can't quite describe. Perhaps, in those moments, I catch a glimpse of the resilience that exists within us all, and that gives me hope.

Through my experiences, I've come to accept that I am sensitive and deeply affected by the world around me. I've always been that way, and I don't believe it's something that can be changed. Instead of viewing it as a weakness, I choose to see it as a strength - a quality that allows me to empathize with others and offer genuine support.

While counseling sessions may have been a valuable tool for some, I found my own way of coping and healing. By sharing my emotions and helping others, I discovered that there is strength in vulnerability and there is healing in extending a hand to those who are hurting. My journey toward healing continues, and in embracing my own path, I hope to inspire others to find their way through the darkness as well.

Throughout this harrowing journey, my mother stood as my anchor of support. Her practicality, understanding, and knowledge were a source of strength during the darkest hours. She was the one person who truly understood me, though I tried to shield her from the depths of my despair.

To those who have experienced similar tragedies, my heartfelt advice is to embrace the emotional turmoil that resides within you. It's okay to feel the pain, to grieve the loss, and to acknowledge the darkness that engulfs your heart. Healing is not a linear journey; it meanders through the depths of grief, acceptance, and hope. Each path is unique, and it's crucial to find your own way forward, even if it means stumbling and faltering along the way.

I wholeheartedly recommend that you allow yourself to experience the full range of emotions, for it is in confronting the pain that you can find the strength to heal and eventually rediscover happiness and laughter. When your heart feels broken and you're on the verge of falling off a cliff, my advice is to take a leap of faith and do things you never thought you could. Challenge yourself every day, even if it's just a tiny step towards healing. The process may be arduous, but it is essential to keep moving forward, no matter how slow the progress.

Drawing from my own experiences, I can attest that navigating the right path is a deeply personal journey. Your mindset and the choices you make ultimately determine where you want to go. Nobody can hold your hand and force you down a particular road. Just as I couldn't impose my healing process on others, you must find your own way and embrace the decisions you make.

There is no one-size-fits-all solution, and it's essential to understand that everyone's healing process is different. You can offer suggestions, new perspectives, and inspiring words, but in the end, the decisions lie with the individual who is healing. Each person has their own inner compass, guiding them towards the path that feels right for them.

I must stress that I am not here to impose my beliefs or preach propaganda. Free will is a precious gift, and it is not my mission to control or direct others. Instead, I strive to teach the importance of mental strength and resilience. Being a supporter means being there for someone during their darkest moments, offering a hand to hold, an ear to listen, and a heart that understands without judgment.

If someone seeks your help, be present for them. Provide a safe space where they can share their emotions without fear or shame. And remember, just like you, they, too, must find their own way through grief and healing. It is not your responsibility to fix them or provide all the answers. Instead, offer your empathy and compassion, and together, you can journey towards a path of healing, understanding, and hope.

As I continue to navigate my own path, I have discovered that the process of healing and finding hope is not about forgetting the past or erasing the pain. It's about accepting the reality of what happened and honoring the memories of those we lost. It's about integrating grief into our lives and finding a way to carry it with us while still embracing the present and future.

Through my own journey, I have learned the importance of resilience, not in the sense of suppressing emotions or putting on a brave face, but in acknowledging that it's okay to stumble, to fall, and to pick yourself back up again. Healing is not about becoming invincible; it's about finding strength in vulnerability and finding light amidst the darkness.

So, to those who have faced tragedies, know that healing is possible. The journey may be daunting, but trust in your inner strength and allow yourself to feel the emotions that come. Reach out to others who can support you on this path, and remember that it's okay to take it one step at a time. Together, we can find hope, solace, and the courage to move forward, embracing life while cherishing the memories of those we've lost.

Grief will ebb and flow like the tide, and it's crucial to be patient with yourself. Challenge yourself every day, even if it means facing fears and confronting past traumas. Allow yourself to laugh, to cry, to find moments of joy amidst the pain.

While I continue to navigate this arduous journey, I have come to understand that closure is not about forgetting or moving on but about integrating the loss into my being. The memories of Travis and Christopher will forever be a part of me, and I cherish them dearly. Their presence will always be felt, and their love will live on in my heart.

In my healing journey, I've found moments of profound transformation and renewal. The process has been arduous, but it has led me to a place of greater strength and resilience. As I continue to carry the memories of Travis and Christopher with me, I am determined to live each day with gratitude, purpose, and unwavering hope.

This is my legacy, a testament to the power of love and the strength of the human spirit. And as I move forward, I hope to inspire others to find their own resilience, seek support, and navigate their own desperate moments with grace and fortitude. For within the depths of despair, there is also the potential for profound healing and hope. And so, with each step forward, I honor the memory of Travis and Christopher and the enduring love that binds us together, forever and always.

CHAPTER 7
COPING WITH LOSS

The weight of the loss settled into my life like a relentless shadow, altering the simplest routines and turning once-ordinary tasks into monumental challenges. It was as if the world had shifted its axis, and I was left stumbling through a reality that was simultaneously familiar and profoundly foreign. The structure of my days seemed hollow, stripped of the purpose and warmth that Travis and Christopher had brought into our home. The laughter that once echoed through the walls was replaced with a haunting silence.

Amid this overwhelming turmoil that had upended my world, the presence of Travis's family and friends became like beacons of unwavering light piercing through the darkness. Their support wasn't just a lifeline; it was an anchor that kept me afloat in the tempestuous sea of grief, preventing me from being consumed by the suffocating waves. In this daunting abyss, one individual, Rob, emerged as an emblem of compassion and understanding that seemed to transcend mere words. Rob, a friend of Travis's, didn't just extend his hand; he reached into the depths of my pain and stood by my side as I attempted to navigate the tumultuous storm of emotions that raged within me. His patient demeanor acted as a soothing balm for my anger and sorrow, offering a refuge where I could be vulnerable without fearing judgment.

Rob's significance was etched into my memory, reminding me of a particular moment that took place right outside my home. This memory was marked by chaos and turmoil, mirroring the tempest within my heart. I recalled an incident where my emotions reached a breaking point, and in a fit of rage, I impulsively flung my solar lights onto the lawn. It was an outward expression of the inner turmoil I was wrestling with. Unexpectedly, Rob was there, calmly collecting the scattered lights without a word. But my emotional storm was far from subsiding, and I found myself erupting once more, my despair manifesting as a frenzy. In the midst of my breakdown, Rob's quiet compassion remained unwavering, providing a sense of stability in the midst of the chaos that had become my life.

Yet, his support wasn't the only one that shone through during this difficult period. Reflecting on the broader tapestry of those who stood by my side, I recognized the role of Travis's friend Robin and other coworkers who offered their guidance. Robin's presence was particularly prominent in the immediate aftermath of the incident.

My emotions, trapped in the anger phase of grief, found an outlet in his understanding presence. It wasn't an easy time for anyone involved, yet his patience and empathy acted as a soothing salve for my wounded spirit.

In the midst of this chaotic tapestry of grief, there were instances where emotions flared, and relationships became strained. Friendships were tested, and at times, even the bonds of understanding were stretched thin. My own emotional landscape was a volatile terrain, and at times, I projected my internal turmoil onto others. In the heat of those moments, it was easy to forget that the individuals around me were navigating their own paths of grief and loss. Through it all, the threads of support and understanding were woven into the fabric of my journey, reminding me that healing was possible even in the face of immense pain and confusion.

The landscape of grief, intricate and multifaceted, revealed itself through unexpected triggers that held the power to transform the mundane into an emotional tempest. In the initial throes of sorrow, a simple trip to a familiar place like Walmart became a labyrinth of pain. The department stocked with children's clothes and playful toys, once innocuous, now became a harrowing passage laden with memories and what-ifs. The mere sight of these items was enough to unravel my composure, triggering a flood of emotions that felt impossible to contain. On that day, as I stood amidst these aisles, the weight of my loss became crushing, and I had no choice but to escape its clutches by walking away, my heart heavy with the agony of what had been taken from me.

Navigating these triggers wasn't merely about avoiding them; it was about acknowledging their existence and working through the emotions they evoked. Like shards of glass scattered along my path, they demanded careful handling. As much as I yearned to shield myself from their impact, I recognized that true healing would only come from confronting them head-on. This realization marked the dawn of a slow but transformative journey. Inching forward, I began to disentangle the threads of association that had wrapped themselves around my heart, binding it to the past.

One profound step on this journey was the difficult decision to release Christopher's ashes from my grasp. The significance of this act was a testament to the depths of my commitment to healing. It wasn't a simple gesture; it was a poignant farewell that carried the weight of all the memories and pain that I had held within me. Entrusting those ashes to the care of Travis's mother was a profound act of letting go, a relinquishing of an anchor that had kept me tethered to a past that had become too painful to bear. As I handed over this physical embodiment of my grief, I understood that it wasn't a betrayal of my love for Christopher. Instead, it was an act of self-preservation, a step toward freeing myself from the gravitational pull of sorrow that had held me captive for so long.

This process of dismantling triggers and letting go of painful relics was neither swift nor linear. It was a symphony of progress and setbacks, of steps forward and moments of regression. It involved recognizing that the scars left by grief would always remain, but they need not dictate my journey. Through the pain, I was slowly cultivating resilience, unearthing the strength to face the triggers, no matter how formidable they seemed. Each act of confronting the past was a testament to my determination to reclaim agency over my emotions to move from a place of vulnerability to one of empowerment.

In the darkest moments, solace often found me in the simplest of activities. Sleep became a refuge, a temporary escape from the overwhelming reality. Yet, my coping mechanisms extended beyond my own struggles. I discovered that reaching out to others, sharing my story, and helping them navigate their own pain brought a sense of purpose to my grief-stricken existence. I longed to spare others the depths of despair I had experienced, and in doing so, I found moments of respite for myself.

The ebb and flow of time ushered in a transformation, turning days into weeks and weeks into months. In the cocoon of my isolation, I sought refuge, a respite from the overwhelming emotions that threatened to engulf me. It was as if I had retreated into a protective shell, shielding myself from the world that had become unbearably complex. Yet, amidst this solitude, I came to a profound realization: the journey toward healing was not one that could be undertaken in isolation.

The threads of connection, frayed but not irreparably broken, began to weave themselves back together. Slowly, almost imperceptibly, I extended tentative bridges toward those who had always been there, waiting in the wings with unwavering support. The isolation I had embraced no longer felt like a sanctuary; it had transformed into a self-imposed exile, one that hindered rather than aided my healing. The familiarity of family and the warmth of friends beckoned me, reminding me that strength lay in unity and that healing could only be fully realized within the embrace of a community that cared.

In the midst of this reawakening, the act of writing this book emerged as an unexpected catalyst for reconnection. The very endeavor that had begun as a solitary expression, a way to exorcise my inner turmoil, morphed into a bridge that spanned the gap between isolation and communion. This book became more than words on a page; it was a lifeline, a thread that connected me to those who had walked alongside me through the darkest of times. In crafting my story, I found not only my voice but also a way to break free from the confines of solitude that had encased me for so long.

The process of sharing my narrative unleashed a powerful catharsis, allowing me to pour out the complexity of my emotions without the filter of external judgment. It was a space where my thoughts flowed unhindered, where I could navigate the labyrinthine corridors of grief with clarity. The act of writing became an instrument of liberation, a channel through which I could speak my truth without the cacophony of well-intentioned but sometimes overwhelming advice. With each stroke of the pen, each tap of the keyboard, I was reclaiming not just my narrative but also my connection to those around me, binding us together in the tapestry of shared experiences.

The indelible memory of Travis and Christopher continues to reverberate through the tapestry of my life, infusing every step I take with their enduring influence. Travis, whose kindness and sweetness were unmatched, left an imprint of patience that I have wholeheartedly embraced. His gentle demeanor and unwavering patience became more than just qualities he possessed; they transformed into lessons etched into the very core of my being. I found myself internalizing his capacity for understanding, drawing strength from his example as I navigated the labyrinth of human interactions. His legacy is a compass that guides me toward embodying empathy, patience, and compassion in my own interactions, a way to honor his memory by perpetuating the kindness he so effortlessly bestowed upon the world.

Christopher's fleeting presence in my life was a revelation that carried the weight of an earthbound angel. His purpose, though brief, was to serve as a catalyst for my growth, a messenger of change and transformation. In his radiant innocence, I discovered a reservoir of strength that I never knew existed within me. Christopher's influence nudged me to evolve, to confront life's challenges head-on, and to find solace in embracing change rather than shying away from it. His ethereal wisdom showed me that adversity could be the crucible from which strength and resilience were forged. Through his presence, I was nudged out of my comfort zone, compelled to shed old layers and emerge as a more resilient and adaptable version of myself.

Travis and Christopher, in their own unique ways, became architects of my character, shaping the blueprint of my life's journey. Their legacies, intertwined with my very essence, continue to light my path as I traverse new avenues and explore fresh horizons. Their stories are not relegated to the past; they are living narratives that propel me forward. I walk not just for myself but as a vessel of their influence, carrying forward the virtues they embodied into new pursuits, forging connections, and seeking perspectives that echo the essence of who they were. In every step I take, their presence is a guiding force, whispering lessons of patience, resilience, and growth into the wind that carries me onward.

The upheaval of loss reshaped the very core of my existence, leading to a metamorphosis of my priorities, values, and aspirations. The landscape of the life I had once known underwent a seismic shift, making way for an unwavering commitment to grasp each fleeting moment and carve out an enduring legacy. A profound sense of purpose stirred within me, a relentless drive to cast aside the shadows of the past and journey towards the horizon of boundless possibilities. It was as if the threads of fate were rewoven into an intricate tapestry of determination and resilience.

This newfound trajectory of mine was born from an unanticipated awakening. The course of my life once assumed to be predictable, took a detour I could never have fathomed. The idea of becoming an author or a producer was, until recently, confined to the realm of dreams. The notion of venturing beyond the comfortable confines of being a housewife contentedly cocooned within the nurturing embrace of familial surroundings, was distant from my thoughts. I reveled in the role of motherhood, cherishing the joys of home life. But the tempestuous storm of loss compelled me to rediscover the spirit of independence that lay dormant within me.

The path I chose was one paved with the audacity of entrepreneurship, a calling I had not previously envisioned. It was an expedition into uncharted waters, an endeavor that promised adventure, growth, and liberation from the chains of a mundane existence. I vehemently resisted the idea of being tethered to a desk, haunted by monotony, and shackled by routine. Instead, I craved the thrill of uncertainty, the exhilaration of embracing the unknown. It was as if life itself beckoned me into its open arms, inviting me to partake in its dance of experiences.

Amidst the swirling currents of transformation, unexpected interests blossomed within my heart. I found myself drawn to the enchanting world of farming. The connection with the land, the rhythm of seasons, and the cycle of growth brought a sense of purpose that I had never anticipated. The fields became a canvas for me to paint my aspirations, each day nurturing life as I nurtured my own healing journey.

There were times when I caught myself gazing wistfully at photographs of riverside camping trips, where laughter and togetherness once flowed like the water itself. Those memories, now both tender and bittersweet, held a nostalgic power over me. Yet, as I stood on the precipice of those moments, the desire to relive them eluded me. The allure of the camping trips that used to be a mainstay of my life now felt like a distant echo, fading against the backdrop of my evolving path.

Amid the changes, the one constant I clung to was the collection of guns that once belonged to Travis. However, even that connection to the past was gradually transforming. I found myself loosening my grip on the physical manifestations of memories, understanding that the true essence of those moments lived within me. It was as if the winds of change were blowing through my life, sweeping away the cobwebs of past identities and making space for the new.

In the midst of rediscovery, I confronted a revelation that echoed with both liberation and trepidation. For far too long, I had existed in the shadows cast by boyfriends and husbands, a shadow that obscured the true contours of my own being. My self-expression had often been an echo of their desires and expectations rather than a genuine reflection of my essence. Now, as I embarked on the journey of self-discovery, I felt the exhilarating rush of unearthing layers of my identity that had remained hidden for too long. It was as if I was piecing together a puzzle, each fragment of my true self falling into place with newfound clarity.

It was not without its challenges. This voyage into self-realization was both thrilling and daunting, akin to venturing into uncharted territory. The prospect of truly embracing my authentic self stirred a blend of excitement and fear within me. Could I become someone I had never truly known before? Could I shed the confines of past roles and expectations to embrace my own aspirations unapologetically? These questions lingered in the corners of my mind, each step forward accompanied by a mixture of courage and vulnerability.

My passions ignited like sparks in the night, fueling a fervent fire within me. The drive to achieve success was no longer just an abstract notion; it was a tangible goal, an aspiration I could actively pursue. As the desire to build a lasting legacy for Ryan and Emma consumed me, the boundaries of what I thought was possible expanded. The vision of mediocrity dissolved in the wake of my ambition. I wasn't content with simply existing; I craved greatness, an impact that would reverberate through time. It wasn't just an external validation I sought but an internal alignment with the force of purpose that now surged through my veins.

With each passing day, the transformation became more evident. Like a phoenix rising from the ashes, I was shedding the remnants of my old self and embracing the radiant potential of the new. The legacy of loss and love intertwined, propelling me toward a future where I could be truly present, fully alive, and relentlessly driven to make a mark on the world.

The pursuit of "normalcy" had always felt like a distant star, forever out of reach in the constellation of my life. Yet, a curious stability began to settle in since the unlikeliest of turns - my transformation into a reverend. This unexpected role, one that I never envisioned for myself, had become a steadfast anchor in the tumultuous sea of my existence. It was as if the pulpit became my refuge, a sanctuary where I could find solace and grounding in the midst of life's tempests.

Being a reverend provided more than a title; it offered me a platform of stability. A haven where I could stand tall, supported by the pillars of faith that had become a part of my identity. The comfort derived from this newfound role was profound, akin to a balm that soothed the wounds of my fractured heart. As I stood before the congregation, my voice carrying echoes of hope and healing, I felt a deep-rooted sense of belonging. The pulpit, once an alien landscape, now held me in its embrace, bestowing upon me a foundation upon which I could rebuild my sense of self.

My role as a reverend wasn't limited to a single faith; it transcended the boundaries of religious labels. It was an invitation to explore the interconnected tapestry of beliefs that formed the rich mosaic of human spirituality. Conversations with individuals from diverse backgrounds became a symphony of perspectives, each note contributing to the melody of understanding. Engaging with followers of different faiths and ideologies revealed a profound truth

- the threads that weave us together are stronger than the divisions that try to pull us apart.

In these exchanges, I found inspiration that transcended dogma and creed. The tapestry of humanity's spiritual quests stretched out before me, a dazzling spectrum of colors and beliefs that were all united by the shared journey of seeking purpose and connection. It was a reminder that we were all part of a greater whole, connected by invisible threads that crisscrossed the expanse of our collective human experience.

However, not all threads were woven with the same intention. The rigidity of closed minds and staunch beliefs gnawed at my spirit. The boxes we constructed around our faiths felt like confining cages, blinding us to the beauty that lay beyond. It saddened me to witness the judgments and prejudices that stemmed from a refusal to acknowledge the common essence that resided within us all. The fervent desire to make people understand that the core of spirituality was not about conformity but about connection burned within me like an unquenchable fire.

As I look back on this chapter of my journey, I see the evolution of a woman who navigated the tides of transformation, embracing the roles that life presented her with. From the depths of loss to the heights of unexpected self-discovery, I had traversed a landscape of emotions and experiences that had shaped me into who I was becoming. The path forward was illuminated by the wisdom of interconnectedness and the light of inclusivity. And so, with an unwavering determination, I continued to walk this path, not as a reverend confined to a pulpit, but as a seeker of truth, a beacon of unity, and a pilgrim on the ever-expanding road of the human spirit.

Part 3

Nurturing Growth

CHAPTER 8

FINDING STRENGTH AND PURPOSE

As I contemplate the intricate tapestry of my journey, the profound personal growth and self-discovery I've encountered emerge as undeniable testaments to the remarkable potency of adversity. Throughout this journey, there were pivotal moments of profound realization that dismantled the veneer of who I believed myself to be. These instances left me wandering through a labyrinth of my own construction, grappling with the depths of my identity. I was ensnared in the intricate weave of the identities others projected onto me, a pattern woven by the expectations of boyfriends and husbands. In this convoluted process, I lost sight of my own essence, obscured by the shadows of their existence. My journey through relationships mirrored a desperate quest to fill the gaping void that loneliness had carved within me.

In terms of self-discovery, I was submerged in an enigmatic labyrinth. I found myself in the perplexing paradox of not knowing who I truly was, perpetually defined by the labels and expectations that others placed upon me. I was entwined in the identities of others, a helpless woman who moved from one relationship to another, perpetually seeking solace outside myself. However, amidst this tumult, I unearthed a pivotal revelation: I am not tethered to another's presence for my own strength. The realization unfurled that I possessed the autonomy to chart my course, to navigate the stormy seas of life unaided. This transformation unveiled the resolute understanding that I am a self-sufficient entity capable of carving my destiny.

My journey into self-discovery unveiled another facet of transformation—a realization that my independence was not merely a philosophical notion. In the throes of longing, my initial yearnings were rooted in the pursuit of comfort, a desire to find solace leaning my head upon another's shoulder. This longing had ensnared me in relationships with individuals whose intentions were far from genuine, propelling me into treacherous waters. It was a pilgrimage through the intricacies of relationships, where I bestowed kindness, warmth, and generosity, only to be met with cruelty and harshness. The labyrinthine nature of these experiences often left me confounded, grappling with the incongruity of my actions and the treatment I received in return. In the wake of these trials, an epiphany blossomed—I comprehended that demons often reach out, clawing to influence our lives in the most unexpected of ways.

As I tie the threads of these experiences together, I see a tapestry of growth that transcends adversity. This journey has led me through the corridors of confusion and the hallways of heartache, but ultimately, it has illuminated the path to rediscovering myself. The shadows of past relationships have begun to disperse, allowing the brilliance of my own light to shine forth. With newfound clarity, I've acknowledged that my self-worth doesn't hinge on the validation of others. I am on a route of self-discovery, exploring the uncharted terrain of my identity, and with each step, I grow more resilient and more resolute. The chrysalis of the past is giving way to the wings of independence, and as I emerge from this transformative cocoon, I carry with me the wisdom that true strength resides within.

It was in the midst of these challenges that I found myself embarking on a journey of helping others who had walked the path of loss. The inspiration to reach out to those who had faced their own tragedies came from a place of deep empathy. I understood the pain, the isolation, and the need for someone to simply listen without judgment. My outreach began with a simple intention: to lend an ear and offer support, sharing my story as a beacon of hope.

Discovering a sense of purpose wasn't like a sudden burst of light illuminating the darkness. Instead, it was a journey that slowly unfolded before me, like a delicate flower revealing its petals one by one. Looking back on the path I've trodden, I see how the struggles and heartaches I endured paved the way for unexpected roles and unexplored passions.

In the midst of life's turbulence, I find myself standing today as a reverend—a role I never envisioned for myself. This unexpected turn of events, like a plot twist in a story, has given me a stable ground from which to reach out and touch lives. It's a platform that allows me to inspire, uplift, and offer solace to those who are seeking a guiding light in their own journeys.

But the journey towards this role wasn't a straight and direct route. It was a path filled with twists and turns, moments of doubt and uncertainty. I remember the first time the idea of becoming a reverend crossed my mind—it felt like a distant dream, something that belonged to another world. Yet, as I embraced this new venture, I found it was a chance to extend my hand to those who were grappling with grief and loss, just as I had.

Another avenue that I've embraced in this chapter of my life is becoming a producer—a realm I never imagined myself entering. The idea of stepping into the world of producing felt like treading on unfamiliar ground, like exploring a foreign land with a compass of curiosity. I was used to being on the receiving end, absorbing stories and experiences. Now, I find myself contributing to the creation of stories, adding my voice to the chorus of storytellers.

This uncharted path of producing has been a revelation. It's allowed me to channel my energy into creative endeavors, into projects that carry messages of hope, resilience, and transformation. It's like nurturing a seed of positivity and watching it sprout into a tree of impact. Each project I take on becomes a testament to the power of storytelling, to the ability of narratives to shape our perspectives and inspire change.

In a way, my journey into producing mirrors my own journey of growth. Just as I've embraced new roles and found purpose in unexpected places, I've come to understand that life's chapters are never written in stone. They're like blank pages waiting for us to pen our stories, to fill them with our experiences, aspirations, and dreams.

Looking back, I realize that this path of purpose and creativity was built upon the foundation of the lessons I learned in the chapters before. The struggles, the pain, and the moments of darkness were all integral to the tapestry of my transformation. They taught me resilience, they taught me to seek light even in the dimmest corners, and they taught me the power of embracing change.

However, as I stepped onto this path of assisting others, challenges emerged. The world can be cruel, and the people within it can sometimes be the very source of the wounds we're trying to heal. But I forged ahead, offering my hand despite the obstacles, determined to make a difference. It's not always an easy road; there have been instances where I've faced resistance and backlash. Religion, in particular, has sometimes been a contentious territory, but I've persevered, unwavering in my commitment to helping others.

Through this mission, I've formed supportive relationships that have brought solace and strength. But vulnerability isn't always easy. I've learned that while some friendships and connections may fall away, the ones that truly matter will endure. Opening up has become a litmus test for authenticity; those who stand by my side, who weather the storms with me, are the ones who truly deserve a place in my life.

As I've embarked on this journey of lending a hand to others, I've encountered a blend of unexpected obstacles and surprising rewards. Amid this path, there have been moments where false accusations, seemingly out of nowhere, have cast a shadow over the purity of my intentions. These unfounded allegations have aimed to tarnish the sincerity of my mission, attempting to obscure the genuine desire to make a positive impact. However, even as I've faced this unwelcome adversity, I've remained resolute in my commitment to the cause.

These experiences have left an indelible mark on my perspective. They've taught me that while change can be met with resistance, it holds the power to usher in profound transformation, both within ourselves and within the larger tapestry of society. It's fascinating how a simple act, born from a place of compassion and genuine care, can ruffle feathers and stir the waters. In a world that often shies away from confronting uncomfortable truths, even the act of raising a voice can spark waves of resistance.

The challenges I've encountered, especially those stemming from the diverse landscape of religious beliefs, have provided me with valuable insights. I've come to realize that my message of compassion and support isn't always embraced by everyone. It's a reminder that the road to progress is often paved with obstacles. Yet, even in the face of these challenges, I'm steadfast in my resolve. I firmly believe that if a message comes from a place of good intentions and authenticity, it's worth weathering the storm of naysayers.

Even when I raise my voice from the mountaintop, calling for unity and understanding, there are moments when the echoes are met with dissent. The reactions of some may question my motives or attempt to cast doubt, yet I remain undeterred. The truth is, my mission isn't about recognition or applause—it's about making a positive difference, no matter how small. Even in the face of backlash and false accusations, my focus remains unwavering: to contribute to a world that is a little more compassionate, a little more supportive, and a little more understanding.

And so, these challenges, though unexpected and often disheartening, have become integral to my journey. They've fortified my dedication to my cause and strengthened my conviction that even the most well-intentioned actions can ruffle feathers. This understanding has infused my perspective with a sense of resilience, reminding me that progress doesn't always come smoothly. As I navigate these uncharted waters, I'm learning to embrace the resistance, face the challenges head-on, and keep moving forward, one step at a time.

The lessons I've learned about resilience, compassion, and our ability to overcome challenges have profoundly impacted how I see the world. As I've reached out to support others, a clear truth has emerged: We all carry our own struggles, our own wounds, and our own unique stories. It's like we're all sailing in the same boat of life, battling our own storms.

Witnessing this truth has shown me the incredible strength of the human spirit. Despite the storms life throws at us, we find ways to hold on and keep moving forward. It's like we're each equipped with an inner resilience that helps us weather even the toughest of times. The struggles we face become part of our shared human experience, weaving a tapestry of challenges and triumphs that connect us all.

Growing up on a ranch, I didn't fully grasp the extent of the challenges people carry. I saw glimpses of it, but I didn't truly understand. However, as I've reached out to others, as I've listened to their stories, my eyes have been opened. I've seen the complexities, the battles that rage within people's hearts and minds. This realization has led me to become more forgiving and more understanding. It's like peering through a window into the depth of human emotions that has taught me to meet others with a compassionate heart.

The truth is, there's no such thing as a perfect life. We all have our struggles, our moments of turmoil. It's like life hands us a mixed bag of joy and pain. If someone tells you they have a life free of challenges, it's like chasing after a mythical creature. It's as rare as finding a unicorn in the wild. So, I've learned to approach people with an open heart, knowing that each person's journey is unique, their battles are real, and their stories are worth hearing.

These profound realizations have molded my perspective. They've etched an unchangeable mark on my outlook. I now approach each person I encounter with a deep understanding that we're all trying to navigate the same unpredictable sea. We all have our oars, our life vests, and our own storms to face. But together, we're not alone in this journey. We're united by our shared experiences and our shared humanity. And in that unity, there's a beauty that transcends the struggles we face.

As I embrace this new chapter of my life, I carry with me the lessons, the pain, and the growth that have shaped me. Accepting my new reality has been a monumental task, one that I've tackled with resilience and a newfound sense of purpose. Through this journey, I've discovered my own strength, my own ability to impact lives, and my own capacity for happiness. As I move forward, I am empowered to continue sharing my story, inspiring others, and building a legacy that honors the memories of Travis and Christopher while embracing the endless possibilities that lie ahead.

CHAPTER 9

EMBRACING THE NEW CHAPTER

As I stand at the threshold of this new chapter in my life, I can't help but reflect on the labyrinth of emotions and experiences that have brought me to this point. The process of finally coming to terms with my new reality and accepting the changes that have occurred has been anything but easy. It's been a rocky journey, a path marked by unexpected twists and turns.

This phase of my life has been like stepping onto a bridge that connects who I was with who I am becoming. It's a process that I'm still navigating, a road that I'm still traveling. Two unexpected careers, production and my role as a reverend, have shaped this new chapter in ways I could have never foreseen.

The journey into production has been a challenging one. It's like trying to navigate a forest without a map. It's an industry that demands not just hard work but a network of connections, and I'm learning that house-kissing, as they call it, is a key ingredient to success. Then there's my path as a reverend, a title that I never imagined I would bear. It's not just a title; it's a passion, a mission to inspire and uplift others. It's also brought its share of challenges. Being a reverend in a world that questions my faith due to my previous atheism has been an interesting paradox. But I've learned to hold onto my beliefs, even in the face of skepticism.

As I conclude this healing journey, the lessons I've learned stand as beacons of guidance. The most pivotal lesson is that I found God. In moments when I could have fallen apart, God has been my anchor. His presence has helped me weather the storms that life has thrown my way. I've discovered a new strength within me, a strength that comes from a higher power. And with that strength, I've embraced my role as a reverend, finding solace in the words I share and the inspiration I offer.

Embracing this new chapter marks a big step in my growth journey. I've changed a lot since I started healing. Realizing that having God in my life is important has really shifted how I see things. It's changed what matters to me, how I look at things, and why I'm here. I've chosen a path that might not be what everyone expects, but it's my way of making a positive difference. I've seen firsthand how being kind can change things, and that's what I want to keep doing.

Finding God has been like finding a rock to lean on when things are tough. It's changed how I understand life. It's not just about me;

it's about everyone. This new understanding has shown me how powerful kindness can be. It's like a ripple effect – one small act of kindness can lead to bigger changes.

This journey has taught me that we're all in this together. We're all part of something bigger. It's not just about me and my path; it's about how we all fit together. This new chapter I'm starting is about sharing the good I've found. It's about helping others and making the world a better place.

Looking back, it's clear that my faith, compassion, and sense of purpose have all grown. This journey has shown me that life's challenges can make us stronger and kinder. And now, as I move forward, I know that I can make a positive impact. It's about shining a light on the good and bringing people together. This journey is about growth, change, and making a difference, step by step. As I look back on the numerous moments that have shaped my journey, there is one particular instance that stands out as a beacon of transformation. It occurred during a time when my life was in flux, amid a move that marked a significant period of change and transition. This instance unfolded in a manner that I could have never predicted, setting into motion a series of events that would profoundly impact my outlook.

In the midst of this move, while navigating the complexities of packing and adjusting to a new environment, I found myself unexpectedly connected with an individual who was in desperate need of assistance. This encounter, seemingly inconspicuous at first, would turn out to be a pivotal turning point, a catalyst that led me to fully embrace the new chapter that was unfolding in my life.

The individual I encountered was a young man, someone who carried the weight of his own struggles. Unbeknownst to me, he was battling the demons of addiction, an inner turmoil that had led him down a treacherous path. Our paths crossed through an unexpected series of events, a door-dashing interaction that took an unforeseen turn. He reached out to me, his tone laced with desperation and a sense of threat, speaking of a halfway house in Salt Lake City, UT as if it were his only refuge. It was at that moment that I decided to step beyond my comfort zone, offering a hand of compassion and support.

As I extended my assistance, I was entering unfamiliar territory. I found myself vigilantly watching over him, acting as a sentinel to ensure that he did not succumb to the temptations of his addiction. My intentions were genuine, and my desire to help him find a better path was unwavering. However, his struggles were more profound than I could have anticipated, and my efforts to shield him from his own demons were met with challenges.

Despite my best efforts, he fell back into the throes of addiction, even while working alongside my own daughter. The experience was a harsh reminder of the complexity of addiction and the battles that individuals like him face. In the midst of this tumultuous journey, the encounter took a deeply disturbing turn. He crossed boundaries that should have never been breached, subjecting me to a traumatic experience that left a lasting mark on my psyche.

In the confines of an Airbnb, I faced an unimaginable ordeal. His actions, fueled by his demons, led to an assault that left me traumatized and bewildered. The pain and fear I endured in those moments left an indelible imprint on my memory. It was as if I had come face to face with a darkness that I had never encountered before. The ordeal left me grappling with feelings of confusion, vulnerability, and a sense of violation that I could not easily shake.

In the aftermath of this terrifying incident, I found myself seeking solace and guidance. I turned to prayer, desperately seeking a sense of peace and understanding in the wake of such an unsettling experience. It was during this time of seeking that I experienced something that defied explanation. A voice, like a guiding whisper, reassured me that I was not alone. It was a moment of divine intervention that provided a glimmer of hope amid the darkness. As I reached out to my mother for support, her efforts to connect with a priest were met with a series of challenges. Yet, even in the face of these difficulties, a voicemail emerged, a message that felt like a lifeline connecting me to a greater source of comfort.

Since that turning point, I've witnessed the tide of change, a calming and restoration of equilibrium. The unsettling presence that once loomed over me has subsided, and a renewed sense of peace has taken its place. I can't help but see this experience as a symbol of the resilience of the human spirit and the power of divine intervention. It's a chapter in my journey that exemplifies the unexpected twists that life can take, leading us down paths we could never have predicted.

This encounter, with all its complexity and emotion, has been a defining factor in my journey of embracing a new chapter. It has solidified my commitment to extending kindness, even when faced with challenges and uncertainty. It's a testament to the transformative power of compassion and the strength we can find in the face of adversity. While the road to embracing this new chapter has been marked by both struggles and triumphs, this moment stands as a poignant reminder that even in the darkest of times, there is a glimmer of light waiting to guide us forward. As I look back at the path I've walked, I can't help but see the threads that connect each moment, each realization. From the darkest depths of grief to the heights of newfound purpose, it's been a journey of resilience, transformation, and rediscovery. Embracing this new chapter isn't just about moving forward; it's about using the lessons learned to light the way for others. I've realized that my journey, with all its ups and downs, can be a source of empowerment for others.

I'm carrying a heart full of hope and a spirit that's eager to inspire. I know that challenges, doubts, and uncertainties are part of the deal. But I'm not letting that stop me. With faith, determination, and a strong wish to make a change, I'm embracing whatever comes my way. This journey has taught me that I can be a source of light, not just for myself, but for those who are also searching for their own healing and growth.

I'll always be grateful for the impact Travis and Christopher had on my life. They've been like guiding lights, even in the toughest times. Their memory pushes me forward. Their patience and courage are qualities I try to have in my own interactions. Christopher's brief presence taught me how to accept change and face challenges head-on. Travis's kindness showed me the importance of being patient and understanding. They've woven into the fabric of who I am, propelling me toward new goals and perspectives. Their legacy continues to be a driving force in my journey.

So, as I take these steps into the new chapter of my life, I carry with me the lessons I've learned, the strength I've gained, and the love I've received. I'm ready to be a light for others, just as Travis and Christopher have been for me. With every challenge I face, every person I help, and every day I embrace, I'm walking forward with gratitude, determination, and a heart that's open to the possibilities ahead.

"The Lord is my light and my salvation; whom shall I fear? The Lord is the stronghold of my life; of whom shall I be afraid?"

Psalm 27:1